This edition published 2015 by The O'Brien Press Ltd.
12 Terenure Road East, Rathgar,
Dublin 6, Ireland
Tel: +353 1 4923333; Fax: +353 1 4922777
E-mail: books@obrien.ie
Website: www.obrien.ie
First published 1974 by Wolfhound Press

ISBN: 978-1-84717-742-1

1 2 3 4 5 6 7 8 9 10
15 16 17 18 19 20

Printed and bound in the Czech Republic by Finidr Ltd.
The paper in this book is produced using pulp from managed forests.

Irish
PROVERBS
& SAYINGS

Irish

PROVERBS
& SAYINGS

SEAMUS CASHMAN
& SEAN GAFFNEY

THE O'BRIEN PRESS
DUBLIN

ACKNOWLEDGEMENTS

We acknowledge with gratitude the contributions and encouragement of many friends, in particular our parents, Ann and James Cashman, and Margaret Gaffney. For their assistance with the original edition of this work, a special word of thanks to Margaret Ryan, Deirdre Duffy, Monica Miller, Joy Adams, John Logue and Paul Walsh. Our thanks also to the artist Billy Merwick from Bandon in County Cork, whose delightful pen and ink illustrations enhanced the many reprintings of the original 1974 edition of this book.

 ABOUT THE AUTHORS

Seamus Cashman is a poet and former book publisher – he founded the Irish literary publishing house, Wolfhound Press, in 1974. He has had several volumes of poetry published; the latest is *The Sistine Gaze* (Salmon Poetry, 2015). Now living in Dublin, he comes from the village of Conna in County Cork.

Sean Gaffney worked in telecommunications in Dublin for several years before returning to his home town of Cavan, where he now lives.

❀ CONTENTS ❀

INTRODUCTION

'The proverb cannot be bettered'; 'though the proverb is abandoned, it cannot be falsified'. How true these are readers will best discover for themselves in the following collection of Irish proverbs, sayings and triads. The triad is perhaps the most fascinating type of saying, and, though little heard today in the non-Irish-speaking parts of the country, it is still to be found in the Gaeltacht areas, especially in West Cork, West Galway and the Aran Islands.

A glance through the index of keywords reveals the range of the Irish proverb, its themes and the imagery and symbols used. As might be expected, the reputed vulnerability of our race to religion and romanticism is well represented. But the story the proverb tells is not quite that of a priest-ridden peasantry content in their poverty. Rather, it shows us to have – or at least to have had – a subtle, sly perhaps, but generally humorous self-confidence. 'The priest's pig' may get 'the most porridge', but the proverb also advises us to be 'neither intimate nor distant with the clergy'! Nor are we shown to be wholly susceptible to romanticism: 'it's better to be lucky than to be an early riser', but 'there's no success without authority and laws'.

The proverbs reveal a deep conviction in a relationship between the spiritual and the material that is both challenging and realistic.

Proverbs are, in a sense, a race's unconscious expression of its moral attitudes. Our proverbs seem frequently to take the form of a national confession of sins: the evils of drink, gambling, greed, vanity, improvidence abound. But the virtues are there: faith, gentleness, love of nature, tolerance and a trust in a life after death that offers a constant check to the materialism already mentioned.

Irish proverbs are rich in nature symbolism and imagery: the wind, the sea, the mountains; plants, animals, birds and fishes. The kingfisher, mackerel, thistle, plover, the horse and the hare, even the common crow are all called upon to mirror our achievements, hopes and failings.

While the proverbs of a race are often readily identifiable as belonging to that race, the ideas expressed and the images used touch on matters more fundamental than a national identity. One can readily accept that Irish proverbs should have their exact counterparts among the proverbs of other Celtic races. There are numerous examples of similarities among the sayings of the Irish, Welsh and Scottish: 'A long illness doesn't lie' (Irish); 'To be long sick and to die nevertheless' (Welsh); 'Marriage at the dungheap and the godparents far away' (Irish); 'Marriage

o'er the anvil, sponsorship o'er the sea' (Scottish); 'A drink is shorter than a story' (Irish and Manx); 'Bribery splits a stone' (Scottish). Such typical proverbs as these also have their counterparts in most European languages.

However, it is interesting to discover that our proverbs also have affinities with those of races as far distant as the West Indies and Africa. Among Jamaican blacks, who are of African descent, there is a saying: 'When you sleep wid darg, you ketch him flea.' Our equivalent is 'He who lies with dogs rises with fleas.' We speak of sending the goose on a message to the foxes' den; the Hausa of West Africa have 'Even if the hyena's town is destroyed, one does not send a dog in to trade.'

Irish proverbs and sayings derive from two main-streams: the Gaelic tradition, in the Irish language, and the Anglo-Irish tradition, in the English language. Both reflect the strong biblical influence found in proverbs throughout 'Western' countries. This collection includes some of the oldest *seanfhocail* (old sayings) recorded in Ireland as well as sayings of more recent origin. But it is by no means exhaustive. The exact origins of most of these sayings are unknown: perhaps a throwaway phrase; perhaps a line of a poem long forgotten – who knows? It is what survives that matters.

For readers interested in pursuing the Irish proverb further, a brief word on some sources. Several substantial

collections have been published (from which many in this collection have been taken, and which we gratefully acknowledge). Most of these are unfortunately long out of print. The most recent, and certainly the finest is T. S. O'Maille, ed., *Sean-fhocala Chonnacht*, 2 vols. (Dublin, 1948–52). Others are: T. O'Donoghue, ed., *Sean-fhocail na Mumhain*, a Gaelic League publication, 1902; E. Ua Muirgheasa, ed., *Sean fhocla Uladh* (1907), which contains English translations, as does T. F. O'Rahilly, *A Miscellany of Irish Proverbs* (Dublin, 1922). Shorter collections will be found in J. O'Daly, *Irish Language Miscellany*; Burke, *Irish Grammar*; Hardiman, *Irish Minstrelsy*, 2 vols., reissued by Irish University Press in 1969; the *Gaelic Journal* and *The Ulster Journal of Archaeology*. P. W. Joyce, *English as We Speak It in Ireland* (Dublin, 1910), is a useful and entertaining starting point though of limited use for proverbs. Two important sources still to be fully researched are the Douglas Hyde 'Diaries' in the National Library of Ireland and the manuscript collections of the Irish Folklore Department in UCD, in particular the 'Schools Mss.' for Anglo-Irish proverbs. *Béaloideas*, the journal of the Folklore Commission, includes lists of proverbs in its various issues. Information on further sources will be found in bibliographies in the published works mentioned.

Most of the proverbs in this collection have been translated from the Irish language. English translations

of proverbs in the Irish language are not always successful. We have endeavoured to remain as close to the original as possible. An illustration of the effects of translation, however, can be readily seen by comparing 'One beetle recognises another' with the original Irish proverb, 'Aithníonn ciaróg ciaróg eile.' The impact of the expression depends greatly on the sound of the word *ciaróg*, and its repetition. The pattern cannot be reproduced satisfactorily in English; and the word 'beetle' is by comparison with the Irish word weak and ineffectual.

We have classified each proverb by subject, recognising that such classification is both limiting and subjective. Proverbs are by their very nature elusive and usually defy adequate classification under any one heading. However, as the index contains the keywords of each proverb, our arrangement should cause the reader little difficulty.

CLASSIFICATIONS

Ability	1–7	Clergy	175–84
Advice	8–14	Coincidence	185
Affectation	15–18	Comfort	186–7
Age	19–27	Compromise	188
Anger	28–31	Contentment	189–90
Appearance	32–8	Conversation	191–3
Art	39	Courtship	194–5
As … as …	40–81	Criticism	196–8
Beauty	82–7	Cunning	199–205
Betrayer	88	Curses	206–14
Bitterness	89	Cynicism	215–16
Blessings	90–100	Danger	217–20
Boasting	101	Death	221–41
Borrowing	102–6	Debt	242–3
Bravery	107–10	Deception	244–50
Bribery	111–14	Delusion	251–4
Carelessness	115–17	Desire	255
Caution	118–44	Despair	256
Change	145–7	Devil	257–60
Character	148	Discipline	261–3
Charity	149–60	Dismissal	264
Chastity	161	Drink	265–84
Children	162–71	Economy	285–6
Choice	172–4	Education	287–91

Effort	292–6	Futility	428–42
Egotism	297	Gambling	443–5
Eloquence	298	Generosity	446–52
Endurance	299	Gentleness	453–4
English, The	300	God	455–68
Equality	301–5	Goodness	469–75
Error	306	Gossip	476–9
Evil	307–12	Gratitude	480–5
Excuses	313–15	Greed	486–95
Experience	316–27	Grief	496–9
Fair-haired	328	Happiness	500
Fame	329–32	Health	501–18
Familiarity	333–6	Home	519–20
Fate	337–46	Honesty	521–4
Fear	347–9	Honour	525–8
Fighting	350–7	Hope	529–41
Flattery	358	Humility	542–3
Flimsiness	359	Humour	544–5
Food	360–5	Hunger	546–51
Fool	366–77	Idleness	552–7
Foolishness	378–82	Ignorance	558
Forgiveness	383	Impossibility	559
Fortune	384–91	Independence	560
Frail	392	Inequality	561–2
Freedom	393–4	Initiative	563–8
Friendship	395–427	Intelligence	569

Involvement	570–2	Obedience	725
Irishman	573–6	Obligation	726
Judgement	577–8	Ownership	727
Justice	579–84	Participation	728
Kerry	585	Patience	729–39
Kindness	586–7	Patriotism	740
Kinship	588–94	Peace	741–7
Knowledge	595–8	Perception	748–9
Law	599–604	Pity	750–1
Laziness	605–17	Poetry	752
Leadership	618	Possession	753–64
Lies	619–21	Poverty	765–85
Life	622–8	Power	786–7
Love	629–46	Presumption	788–93
Luck	647–54	Pride	794–9
Manners	655–6	Procrastination	800–2
Marriage	657–78	Promise	803
Maturity	679	Proverbs	804–6
Meanness	680–5	Prudence	807–9
Men	686	Red Hair	810–11
Misfortune	687–96	Repentance	812–13
Mother	697–9	Reputation	814–17
Nature	700–17	Revenge	818
Neatness	718	Rogue	819–23
Necessity	719–23	Rumour	824–7
Nobility	724	Scarcity	828–30

Seasons	831–5	Warning	932
Secret	836–43	Wastefulness	933
Self-destruction	844–7	Wealth	934–43
Selfishness	848–53	Weather	944–6
Sense	854	Welcome	947–9
Separation	855	Widow	950
Shame	856–8	Wisdom	951–62
Shyness	859–60	Women	963–93
Silence	861–8	Work	994–1022
Strength	869	Youth	1023–8
Stupidity	870–2		
Success	873–4		
Suitability	875–7		
Tact	878–87		
Talent	888–91		
Talkativeness	892–4		
Thrift	895–7		
Time	898–900		
Treachery	901–2		
Trouble	903–4		
Trust	905–6		
Truth	907–17		
Understanding	918–19		
Uselessness	920–4		
Value	925–8		
Vanity	929–31		

ABILITY

No one can tell what he is able to do till he tries   no. 1

You can't whistle and chew meal at the same time   2

You can't bark and run at the same time   3

A vessel only holds its fill   4

Often the hound that was made fun of killed the deer   5

The strong man may when he wants to; the weak man
     when he's able   6

The *gobadán* (kingfisher) cannot work both tides   7

ADVICE

Don't give cherries to pigs; don't give advice to a fool   8

A man is often a bad adviser to himself and a good
     adviser to another   9

The man who won't have advice will have conflict   10

He is bad that will not take advice, but he is a
     thousand times worse that takes every advice   11

The cat is his own best adviser   12

Crafty advice is often got from a fool   13

A wise man takes advice   14

AFFECTATION

A ring on her finger and not a stitch of clothes on her back   15

Sparing at home and lavish in the hospital   16

Like the sun on the hill-top, but like a thistle on the
    hearth   17

Street angel, house devil   18

AGE

When the twig hardens, it's difficult to twist it   19

A man lives long in his native place   20

It's hard to teach an old dog to dance   21

As the cock crows, the young bird chirrups   22

To be old and decayed dishonours no one   23

In youth we have our troubles before us in age we
    leave pleasure behind   24

Young people don't know what age is; old people forget
    what youth was   25

The old man hasn't the place of the cat in the ashes   26

Is it not a lonesome thing to be getting old?   27

ANGER

There's anger in an open laugh   28

Old burdens don't incite blows   29

Red-hot ashes are easily rekindled   30

No wrong to be done to seven classes of persons
    excited to anger: a bard, a chief, a woman, a
    prisoner, a drunken person, a druid and a king in
    his own dominions   31

APPEARANCE

An inch is a great deal in a man's nose   32

It's not the bones that are beautiful but the flesh on the shoulders   33

A thong is no shorter for having been in water   34

Its appearances are better than its value   35

Handsome is as handsome does   36

A black hen lays white eggs   37

A buckle is a great addition to an old shoe   38

ART

Nobility listens to art   39

AS ... AS

As stiff as a poker   40

As tough as a wheelstring   41

As mim as a dog without his tail   42

As black as Toal's cloak   43

As bad as Barrington's bloodhound to us   44
A localised Kerry expression. When the Irish were being hunted down in Penal times, a particularly vicious duo, a Captain Barrington and Colonel Nelson, used a bloodhound to chase their quarry which savaged the victim terribly, hence giving rise to the saying

As old as Atty Hayes' goat 45

A Cork expression. The story goes that the goat belonged to Atwell Hayes who was father of Sir Henry Hayes, sheriff of Cork in 1790. The goat was reputed to be old even when Atty was a young man. A generation later, Captain Philip Allen, son-in-law of Sir Henry Hayes became mayor of Cork (in 1800) and gave a civil banquet to celebrate the occasion. At this time the goat died, and Allen, being a bit of a joker, served up the hind quarters of the goat unknowingly to his guests, as venison. The 'venison' was proclaimed delicious by the city fathers. In County Armagh, the corresponding expression is 'as old as Killylea bog'

As wise as the woman of Mungret 46

A Limerick expression. The very amusing story attached to this saying concerns the monastic foundation and school at Mungret. A number of scholars were sent from Cashel to compete with their Mungret counterparts. However, the Limerick scholars, fearing defeat and the loss of their reputation, dressed as washerwomen and waited along the roadside, washing in the nearby river. As the Cashel contingent approached and asked the 'women' for directions, they were completely taken aback when answered in perfect Greek. Thinking that if the washerwomen were so learned then the scholars must be unusually brilliant, the poor Tipperary monks turned for home, leaving the reputation of Mungret intact and untarnished!

As hard as the hob of Hell   47

As cunning as the fox   48

As long as a wet Sunday   49

As old as the hills   50

As bald as a *buailtín* (*see notes*)   51

As sharp as a *ciotóg* (*see notes*)   52

As bitter as thick milk   53

As crooked as a ram's horn   54

As brown as a berry   55

As big as a smith's *meitheal* (*see notes*)   56

As sharp as the word of a fool   57

As sharp as the teeth of a hound   58

As wet as dung   59

As pretty as a May flower   60

As old as the Cailleach Beare (*see notes*)   61

As fresh as a daisy   62

As bright as a lily   63

As slow as a late dinner   64

As dull as ditchwater   65

As swift as a hare   66

As true as the gospel   67

As deep as the sea   68

As bashful as a girl   69

As treacherous as an Englishman   70

As melodious as a lark   71

As brave as Fionn mac Cumhaill (*see notes*)   72

As yellow as a ragweed (ragworth)   73

As lazy as a donkey   74

As lazy as a piper's *luidín* (little finger)   75

As busy as a bee   76

As salty as the sea 77

As good as gold 78

As rich as Damer 79

A Dublin expression, not in common usage. The story is based on Joseph Damer who was born in 1630. After serving Cromwell he returned to Ireland where he purchased much land forfeited in the Williamite confiscations. He became a banker and achieved much notoriety as a miser. He died in 1720, leaving nearly half a million pounds, a phenomenal amount even by today's standards. Jonathan Swift was moved, as was his wont, to comment unfavourably on Mr. Damer:

> *The ghost of old Damer who left not his betters*
> *When it heard of a bank appear'd to his debtors*
> *And lent them for money the backs of his letters*
> *His debtors they wonder'd to find him so frank,*
> *For old Nick gave the papers the mark of the bank*

As hairy as a puck-goat's head 80

As thieving as a fox's snout 81

BEAUTY

Irish beauty … a woman with two black eyes 82

Beauty won't make the pot boil 83

Beauty is only skin deep 84

Beauty suffers no pain 85

It's the jewel that can't be got that is the most beautiful 86

The man without eyes is no judge of beauty 87

BETRAYER

Woe to him whose betrayer sits at his table   88

BITTERNESS

A mouth of ivy and a heart of holly   89

BLESSINGS

May the Lord keep you in his hand and never close
    his fist too tight on you   90

May we have the grace of God and may we die in Ireland   91

May you live and wear it   92

May you have health to wear it   93

May luck be to the married couple   94

May the face of every good news and the back of every
    bad news be towards us   95

May your voice be above every voice   96

May the strength of three be in your journey   97

May I see you grey and combing your children's hair   98

May I see you in Heaven   99

God bless three times, and three spits for luck   100
    (said at the birth of a calf)

BOASTING

There are two heads on all his sheep   101

BORROWING

The law of borrowing is to break the borrower 102

The borrowed horse has hard hooves 103

The loan of something on loan 104

Don't exchange your horse when you are crossing
the river 105

He who is bad to give the loan is good for directing
you 106

BRAVERY

The brave man never loses 107

Every dog is valiant at his own door 108

Every hound is brave on his own dunghill 109

Every man is bold until he faces a crowd 110

BRIBERY

Bribe the rogue and you need have no fear of the
honest man 111

Beware of the bribed man 112

Bribery will split a stone 113

Hold on to the bone and the dog will follow you 114

CARELESSNESS

Loose and careless like the leg of a pot 115

A ship is often lost because of one man   116

By their tongues people are caught, and by their
horns, cattle   117

CAUTION

Never reach out your hand further than you can
withdraw it   118

A look in front is better than two behind   119

Don't see all you see and don't hear all you hear   120

Leave well enough alone   121

Don't show all your teeth until you can bite   122

The first sip of broth is always the hottest   123

Kill a wren but beware of fire   124

Be first in a wood but last in a bog   125

Think before you speak and look before you leap   126

Better be sure than sorry   127

He that doesn't tie a knot will lose the first stitch   128

When your hand is in the dog's mouth, withdraw
it gently   129

If you catch a pig catch it by the leg   130

Don't be breaking your shin on a stool that's not in
your way   131

Never scald your lips with another man's porridge   132

Look at the river before you cross the ferry   133

A stitch in time saves two stitches   134

Better to turn back from the middle of the ford
   than to be drowned in the flood   135

When your neighbour's house is on fire, take care of
   your own   136

A person often ties a knot with his tongue that can't
   be loosed by his teeth   137

One look before is better than three looks behind   138

Don't put your hook in a field without being asked   139

Never take the full of your mouth out of anybody   140

Say little and say it well   141

Put a mouth to a mouth, but don't put a pen to paper   142

Least said soonest mended   143

No falling out with a madman   144

CHANGE

A change of work is as good as a rest   145

The new broom sweeps the house best   146

The black countenance (pessimist) cannot be changed   147

CHARACTER

A good man is not without fault and there are two
   faults in any man   148

Charity

He who is bad at giving a lodging is good at showing
the road 149

Constant begging meets only constant refusal 150

A shut fist gets only a closed hand 151

No good is got from waste, but a good name is got
by alms-giving 152

Half given is better than complete refusal 153

The good deed boasted of is little; the good deed
not acknowledged is little better 154

Better to do a good deed and boast about it than not
to do it and not boast about it 155

Words will not feed the friars 156

Don't postpone the good deed 157

It is a little thing that is not longer than your hand 158

Charity begins at home 159

Water for the goose and alms for the beggar 160

Chastity

The beauty of a chaste woman makes bitter words 161

Children

Praise the child and it will progress 162

If they won't make you laugh, they won't make you cry 163

A wise son makes a father glad but a foolish son is a
    mother's sorrow   164

Baptise your own child first   165

Every finger has not the same length, nor every son the
    same disposition   166

What the child sees is what the child does   167

Every mother thinks it is on her own child the sun rises   168

An inch of a lad is better than a foot of a girl   169

No man ever wore a cravat as nice as his own child's
    arm around his neck   170

Your son is your son today, but your daughter is your
    daughter forever   171

Choice

If the bare part of the hill is bad, the summit is worse   172

It can't be both curds and whey with you   173

It's difficult to choose between two blind goats   174

Clergy

The priest's pig gets the most porridge   175

Although there was nobody present but the priest
    and the friar, still I have lost all my property   176

A dumb priest never got a parish   177

If there is a hen or a goose it's surely on the priest's
    table it will be   178

It is his own child the priest baptises first   179

Be neither intimate nor distant with the clergy 180

A priest that's made a pet of and a pig that's made a
pet of are the two worst pets of all 181

The way of the nuns with the countrywomen – they
receive a great lump and give a small return 182

Give the priest his own side of the road 183

Don't be mean and don't be generous with the clergy 184

COINCIDENCE

Talk of the Devil and he will appear 185

COMFORT

Tobacco after food 186

When the belly is full, the bones like to stretch 187

COMPROMISE

Bend with the tree that bends with you 188

CONTENTMENT

A share is sufficient 189

A little fire that warms is better than a big fire that burns 190

CONVERSATION

It's better to tell a good story twice 191

There's no tax on talk   192

Talk is cheap   193

COURTSHIP

When you go forth to find a wife, leave your eyes at
    home but take both ears with you   194

It's the last suitor that wins the maid   195

CRITICISM

A good horseman is the man on the ground   196

He's a good hurler that's on the ditch   197

The one who loses the game has the liberty of talking   198

CUNNING

He would cover a rock with hay and sell it for a haycock   199

He would skin a louse and send the hide and fat to
    market   200

He would build a nest in your ear   201

In spite of the fox's cunning, his skin is often sold   202

He'd steal the cross off an ass's back   203

He would steal the egg from the crane and finally
    the crane herself   204

Cunning is better than strength   205

CURSES

The curse does not fall on a stick or a stone   206

A bad death to you   207

Bad cess to you (*see notes*)   208

A heart-burning on you   209

A cold day on you   210

The raven's curse on you   211

The kitten's death to you   212

May your trouble be in your throat   213

The curse of Cromwell on you   214

CYNICISM

It's a very good time if it lasts   215

When the sky falls we'll all catch larks   216

DANGER

The man who loves danger shall perish in it   217

No staying in dangerous roads   218

A lion is not a safe companion for all persons   219

A horse on a cliff or a cow in a swamp, two in danger   220

DEATH

Many a day we shall rest in the clay   221

Death is the poor man's best physician   222

Death doesn't come without a cause   223

There's neither herb nor cure for death   224

To die and to lose one's life are much the same thing   225

There'll be many a dry eye at his death   226

There is hope from the mouth of the sea but none from the mouth of the grave   227

A man at sea may return but not the man in the churchyard   228

Sleep is the brother (or the image) of death   229

One can't tell which skin will hang from the rafter first, the old sheep's or the lamb's   230

The trace of the hand will live but not the hand that made it   231

Death stares the old in the face and lurks behind the backs of the young   232

Nimble as the hare is, she is caught at last   233

There is many a person with a high head today who will be lying lowly tomorrow   234

May God spare anyone who has a hand in his own death   235

You will never comb a grey head   236

It is not the tree that is a long time shaking that is the first to fall   237

Death does not take a bribe   238

The graveyard growth is in him   239

Death never comes too late 240

You'll be going yet and your two feet before you 241

DEBT

Better old debts than old grudges 242

Forgetting a debt doesn't pay it 243

DECEPTION

There is often a barb behind a kiss 244

A lie looks the better for having a witness 245

A sweet tongue is seldom without a sting to its root 246

Shallow waters make great noise 247

Still waters run deep 248

Show the fatted calf but not the thing that fattened him 249

One swallow never made a summer 250

DELUSION

Faraway cows have long horns 251

Lying in lavender like Paddy's pig 252

Them that like the dunghill see no motes in it 253

It's not as one supposes that things are 254

DESIRE

Desire conquers fear 255

DESPAIR

It is often there has been great darkness with little
    rain   256

DEVIL

Never bid the Devil good morrow until you meet him   257

To praise God is proper – but a wise man won't
    blackguard the Devil   258

Needs must when the Devil rides   259

The man of horns is active   260

DISCIPLINE

A crooked cane makes a straight back   261

There is no achievement without discipline   262

The horse wins or loses the reins   263

DISMISSAL

The back of my hand and the sole of my foot to you   264

DRINK

A drink is shorter than a story   265

There's little profit from being always drunk   266

It's the first drop that destroyed me, there's no harm
    at all in the last   267

It [whiskey] would make a rabbit spit at a dog   268

He would go to mass every morning if holy water
   were whiskey   269

You take your health once too often to the whiskey
   shop till it gets broken   270

It's sweet to drink but bitter to pay for it   271

Sweet is the wine but sour's the payment   272

Wine reveals the truth   273

Thirst after the drink and sorrow after the money   274

Drunkenness will not protect a secret   275

The cure of the drinking is to drink again   276

Thirst is a shameless disease   277

Donal drunk and his wife drinking water   278

He would drink Lough Sheelin dry (*see notes*)   279

It is only folly to treat an old woman to a dram   280

When good luck comes the drink comes   281

A drunken woman is lost to shame   282

Thirst begets thirst   283

The end of drinking is more thirst   284

ECONOMY

Take what you can get and pay what you can   285

Economy is good to guard against want, but don't
   be mean or niggardly   286

EDUCATION

Though I have the book I don't have the learning   287

A man of learning understands the half-word   288

Learning is a light burden, but often a source of
    confusion   289

Every pupil as he is taught   290

The young and the foolish are the hardest to teach   291

EFFORT

Better a good run than a long standing   292

One's best is sufficient   293

A hook well lost to catch a salmon   294

Often a man cast a sprat to catch a hake   295

If you stretch out with your hand, you will reach out
    with your feet   296

EGOTISM

Speak neither well nor ill of yourself   297

ELOQUENCE

There is no bone in the tongue, but it often broke
    a man's head   298

ENDURANCE

Even a good horse can't keep running   299

THE ENGLISH

Don't yield to the Saxon but beat him well   300

EQUALITY

A cat can look at a king   301

The beak of the goose is no longer than that of the
gander   302

Right for me, right for you   303

The river is no wider from this side or the other   304

In the land of the blind, the man with one eye is a
king   305

ERROR

A slip of the tongue is no fault of the mind   306

EVIL

Evil may spring from the tiniest thing   307

The effects of an evil act are long felt   308

The more you trample dung the more it spreads   309

A small stain will smear white stockings   310

The bad deed turns on its doer   311

Evil begets evil   312

EXCUSES

The losing horse blames the saddle   313

A bad reaper never got a good reaping hook   314

It's a bad thing not to have some story on the tip of
    your tongue   315

EXPERIENCE

A burnt child fears the fire   316

Be one's trade good or bad, experience makes one a
    master of it   317

The wearer knows best where the shoe pinches   318

The proof of the pudding is in the eating   319

On an unknown path every foot is slow   320

Let every man praise the ford as he finds it   321

An old bird is not caught with chaff   322

The longest road out is the shortest road home   323

An old cat will not burn himself   324

Sense bought (i.e. experience) is better than two
    senses learned   325

You can't put an old head on young shoulders   326

Every hound is a pup till he hunts   327

FAIR-HAIRED

If I am yellow I have a fair heart   328

FAME

Fame lasts longer than life   329

Without money fame is dead   330

Falling is easier than rising   331

Greatness knows modesty   332

FAMILIARITY

To know somebody, (one must) live in the same house
    with them   333

Too much of one thing is the same as nothing   334

Familiarity breeds contempt   335

People of the same trade are friendly   336

FATE

Long as the day may be, night comes at last   337

He that is born to be hanged needn't fear water   338

Every nursling as it is nursed, every web as it is woven   339

Pity the man drowned in the storm; for after the rain
    comes the sunshine   340

The darkest hour is nearest dawn   341

A ship is often lost by the harbour   342

No matter how often a pitcher goes to the water,
   it is broken in the end   343

No matter how long the day, night comes   344

What kills one man gives life to another   345

About the foot of the tree the foliage falls   346

FEAR

Fear is a fine spur; so is rage   347

Be afraid, and you'll not meet danger   348

The man who is struck on the head, will afterwards
   be afraid   349

FIGHTING

To fight like Kilkenny cats   350

In 1798 when the Hessians were quartered in Kilkenny they amused themselves by tying two cats' tails together and throwing them over a line, to fight. Their officer on hearing of this, ordered his men to stop. However, the soldiers continued the practice in secret, and one day while they were amusing themselves in this manner they heard the officer approaching. One soldier drawing his sword cut down the cats leaving only their tails hanging. When the officer enquired as to where the cats were, the soldier replied that the cats had fought so furiously they had devoured all but each other's tails. The story proved immensely popular and achieved widespread fame, but it is probably just a tall tale!

Quarrelsome dogs get dirty coats   351

Don't kick till you're spurred   352

Be warning but not striking   353

A word goes to the wind but a blow goes to the bones   354

Wine is better than blood   355

There is often the death of a person between two words   356

Don't go between the tree and its bark   357

FLATTERY

Soft words butter no parsnips   358

FLIMSINESS

The sheep could eat the grass through it   359

FOOD

The juice of the cow alive or dead is good   360

Help is a good thing except at the table of food   361

A man at the food and a weakling at the work   362

First at the pot and last at the work   363

Food is a workhorse   364

Taste the food and you'll get a taste for it   365

FOOL

A fool and his money are easily parted   366

A fool's word is a thorn in the mud   367

When fools make mistakes they lay the blame on
Providence   368

It's a trifle that makes fools laugh   369

Give a clown his choice and he'll chose the worst   370

Gold is light with a fool   371

Give me that and be a fool yourself   372

There's no fool like an old fool   373

Often a fool's son is a wise man   374

The *amadán* (male fool) fell into the fire and the
oinseach (female fool) began to cry   375

The fool has luck   376

The *oinseach* sees the *amadán*'s faults   377

FOOLISHNESS

She burnt her coal and didn't warm herself   378

Hurry no man's cattle … get a jackass for yourself   379

Don't take the thatch off your own house to buy slates
for another man's roof   380

Folly has a fall before it   381

There are two things that cannot be cured: death,
and want of sense   382

FORGIVENESS

Forgive a horse that will cock his ears   383

FORTUNE

Good luck is better than early rising   384

Fortune is a good thing, but it's worth searching for it   385

The ugly are often lucky and the handsome unfortunate   386

Often does the likely fail and the unlikely prosper   387

It is a bad wind that doesn't blow for someone   388

Prosperity often comes to the easygoing   389

The lucky man awaits prosperity, the unlucky man
gives a blind leap   390

Let each person judge his own luck, good or bad   391

FRAIL

The point of a rush would draw blood from his cheek   392

FREEDOM

Let every man have his own world   393

You can take the horse to the well, but you can't make
him drink   394

FRIENDSHIP

No war is as bitter as a war between friends, but it
doesn't last long   395

Reverence ceases once blood is spilled   396

Two persons never lit a fire without disagreeing   397

If you will walk with lame men you will soon limp
    yourself   398

There was never a scabby sheep in a flock that didn't
    like to have a comrade   399

The man long absent is forgotten   400

In times of trouble friends are recognised   401

A friend's eye is a good mirror   402

Reckoning up is the ending of friendship   403

The friend that can be bought is not worth buying   404

If I like the sow I like her litter   405

Prove your friend before you need him   406

A little relationship is better than much friendship   407

Take care but take no sides and on no account sacrifice
    your friends   408

Pick your company before you sit down   409

Tell me who your friends are and I'll tell you who
    you are   410

A friend in court is better than a penny in one's purse   411

Friendship is good though separation is painful   412

Cook a little spit for me and I'll cook one for you   413

As well whistle jigs to a milestone as tell troubles to you   414

Friends are better than gold   415

A constant guest is never welcome   416

Don't show your skin to the person who won't cover it   417

The people will meet but the hills and mountains never   418

The coldness of a friend is better than the sweetness of
    an enemy   419

He who lies with dogs rises with fleas   420

It is better to be alone than to be in bad company   421

Be kind with the wretched but dark and dour to your
    enemy   422

When the hand ceases to scatter, the mouth ceases
    to praise   423

A little help is better than a deal of pity   424

Don't put your friend in your pocket   425

A shoulder without a kinsman (friend) is bare,
    and woe to him who lacks a loving brother   426

Pity the man in a country where there is none to take
    his part   427

FUTILITY

Putting the thatch of the kiln on the mill   428

It's like looking for a hound without knowing its
    colour   429

To address a head without knowledge is like the
    barking of a dog in a green valley   430

You might as well talk to the wall as to him   431

Don't waste your breath on dead embers   432

A nod is as good as a wink to a blind horse   433

It's no use going to the goat's house to look for wool   434

It's hard to fight with the wide ocean   435

An empty bag won't stand 436

'Tis hard to drive a hare out of a bush he's not in 437

You can't draw blood out of a turnip 438

You won't make a rope from the sand of the sea 439

It's only the Lord can make a racehorse out of a jackass 440

The Devil couldn't do it unless he was drunk 441

'Tis no use talking when the harm is done 442

GAMBLING

It is the hope of recompense that ruins the card-player 443

Better a son a gambler than a drinker 444

The expectation of success is what beggars the gambler 445

GENEROSITY

A big belly was never generous 446

A generous man, they say, has never gone to Hell 447

Wide is the door of the little cottage 448

As you have burned the candle, give the inch 449

Take gifts with a sigh, most men give to be paid 450

O'Neill's gift and his two eyes looking after it
(see notes) 451

It is worth going to meet generosity that is slow 452

GENTLENESS

A gentle answer quenches anger   453

A kind word never broke anyone's mouth   454

GOD

God's help is nearer than the door   455

God is not as severe as he is said to be   456

God often pays debts without money   457

God moves slowly yet his grace comes   458

God never closes one door but he opens another   459

God shares the good things   460

The person not taught by God is not taught by man   461

The love of God guides every good   462

Man talks but God directs   463

God helps him that helps himself   464

The will of God yesterday, today and forever   465

The grace of God is between the saddle and the ground   466

God made the back to suit the burden   467

Whatever God has allotted me I cannot sell   468

GOODNESS

Do good in the face of evil   469

The good that is, is better than two goods that were   470

He has a good heart even if he is sallow   471

The good is never late   472

Everything good is used in little pieces   473

A good thing is improved by increasing it   474

Good begets good   475

GOSSIP

A whisper in Nora's ear is louder than a shout from the highest hill   476

A woman told me that a woman told her that she saw a woman who saw a woman who made ale of potatoes   477

The death of the old woman and the marriage of the young woman   478

Talk by the fire is the talk of idle women   479

GRATITUDE

Sit on your heel and thank goodness for a new stool   480

You can't examine the teeth of a gift horse   481

Eaten bread is soon forgotten   482

I think little of buttermilk when I'm full of it   483

Strike a dog with a bone and he'll not growl   484

Thank God the right side of the house is out   485

GREED

One cannot take out of a sack more than the full of it   486

If the cat had a churn her paw would often be in it   487

Though honey is sweet, do not lick it off a briar   488

The covetous man is always in want   489

He's not covetous but he'd fain have all   490

Don't refuse to sell your horse for the sake of a crown   491

Eating and complaining like the greedy hen   492

A rag on every bush   493

Too many irons in the fire   494

A finger in every pie   495

GRIEF

The most recent grief is the heaviest   496

No grief at feasts   497

From strong relationships often comes great grief   498

There is no cure for grief but to put it under your foot   499

HAPPINESS

There is no happiness without an inch of sorrow
through it   500

health

The herb that can't be got is the one that brings relief   501

A good laugh and a long sleep, the best cures in a
     doctor's book   502

Sickness is the physician's feast   503

The beginning of a ship is a board, of a kiln a stone,
     of a king's reign salutation, and the beginning of
     health is sleep   504

A long disease doesn't tell a lie; it kills at last   505

Health is better than wealth   506

Health is better than flocks   507

A healthy man is a king   508

The relapse is worse than the final fever   509

Every patient is a doctor after his own cure   510

What butter or whiskey will not cure, there's no cure
     for   511

A long illness doesn't lie   512

Beginning with a cough and ending with a coffin   513

A graveyard cough   514

The person who doesn't scatter the morning dew will
     not comb grey hairs   515

One must pay health its tithes   516

The physician's hope, every misfortune   517

Patience is the cure for an old illness   518

home

There is no fireside like your own fireside   519

It's a long way from home that the plover cries   520

honesty

When rogues disagree, honest men get their own   521

The man that steals stacks thinks all the world thieves   522

The miller's pigs are fat but God knows whose meal
they ate   523

He is as honest as the priest   524

honour

A patch is better than a hole, but a hole is more
honourable than a patch   525

It's more difficult to maintain honour than to become
prosperous   526

A man may live after losing his life but not after losing
his honour   527

Honour is more precious than gold   528

hope

Live horse and you'll get grass   529

Hope soothes the tired heart   530

Hope is the physician of each misery   531

Face the sun but turn your back on the storm 532

There's no flood that doesn't recede 533

Do not expect more than you deserve 534

God never sent a mouth without something with it 535

The dogs have not eaten up the end of the year yet 536

Good hope is better than a bad intention 537

There are fish in the tide as good as any that has been taken 538

There's fish in the sea better than was ever caught 539

In the end the improvement comes 540

The night and the day are as long as ever they were 541

HUMILITY

The last place is worthy of the best loved 542

The heaviest ear of corn is the one that lowest bends its head 543

HUMOUR

Good humour comes from the kitchen 544

Crying is not far away from laughter 545

HUNGER

It's a good story that fills the belly 546

Hunger is a good sauce 547

The mountain is a good mustard 548

The hungry hound thinks not of her whelps 549

Sharp is the eye of the hungry person 550

A blessing does not fill the stomach 551

IDLENESS

Talking never brought the turf home 552

Don't let the grass grow under your feet 553

Better idle than working for nothing 554

It is better to be putting knots on a straw than to be idle 555

A foot at rest meets nothing 556

You have the foal's share of the harrow 557

IGNORANCE

No ignorance in ordinance or law 558

IMPOSSIBILITY

The rod impossible to twist 559

INDEPENDENCE

Do your own job and eat your own fruits 560

INEQUALITY

What's rent to a lord is food to a child   561

A king's shilling is no more than a poor man's farthing   562

INITIATIVE

The army that attacks will not be attacked   563

The ebb-tide won't wait for the slow man   564

A shut fist will not catch a hawk   565

Strike the ball when you get it on the hop   566

Strike while the iron is hot   567

The man without resourcefulness is no better than a pig   568

INTELLIGENCE

A spur in the head is worth two on the heel   569

INVOLVEMENT

In for a penny, in for a pound   570

You might as well be hung for a sheep as a lamb   571

An inch is as good as a mile   572

IRISHMAN

An Irishman carries his heart in his hand   573

Put an Irishman on the spit and you'll find two more
    to turn him   574

An Irishman is never at peace except when he's fighting   575

The Irishman is impatient   576

JUDGEMENT

Don't make little of your dish for it may be an ignorant
    fellow who judges it   577

Disputation in the heel of judgement   578

JUSTICE

No merriment in the seat of justice   579

Innocent or guilty, he'll be hanged said the judge   580

There is little between justice and injustice   581

Put justice before generosity   582

Those who make laws should not break laws   583

What is got badly goes badly   584

KERRY

Kerry security: bond, pledge, oath, and keep the money   585

KINDNESS

Pressure of the business weakens kindness   586

The old hag is the better of being warmed, but the worse
    of being burned   587

KINShIP

One beetle recognises another   588

Blood is stronger than water   589

One chafer knows another   590

One thief knows another   591

One pig knows another   592

One liar knows another   593

Great minds live apart, people may meet, but mountains
    and rocks never   594

KNOWLEDGE

A blind dog won't bark at the moon   595

A book to a blind man signifies nothing   596

Better knowledge of the evil, than the evil without
    knowledge   597

The person with least knowledge talks most   598

LAW

It's no joke going to law with the Devil and the court
    held in Hell   599

Beyond the leap, beyond the law   600

A good word in court is better than a pound in the
   purse   601

Neither break a law nor make one   602

The law does not apply to the blow that's not struck   603

The lying man's witness is his wife   604

LAZINESS

Winter comes fast on the lazy   605

Cold in the shoulder makes the shins speckled (*see notes*)   606

Long sleep makes a bare backside   607

It's only a worthless hen that fails to provide for herself   608

The speckled shins of spring is the envious one in
   autumn (*see notes*)   609

Laziness is a heavy burden   610

You'd be a good messenger to send for death   611

Pity the man who waits till the last day   612

Ye look for the ladle when the pot's in the fire   613

The long stitch of the lazy tailor   614

A slow messenger is the better for your going to meet
   him   615

It's a bad bird that dirties its own nest   616

It's a bad hen that won't scratch herself   617

LEADERSHIP

After the chieftains fall, the fight seldom continues   618

LIES

As great a liar as the clock of Strabane   619

The lie often goes further than the truth   620

God does not like the lying tongue   621

LIFE

We live as long as we're let   622

You will live during the year for we were just talking
   of you   623

Life is sweet   624

Life is precious   625

People live in one another's shadows   626

Twenty years agrowing; twenty years at rest; twenty
   years declining; and twenty years when it doesn't
   matter whether you're there or not   627

Life is the true historian   628

LOVE

Live in my heart and pay no rent   629

If you love the mother, you love her brood   630

They won't fall in love with the man they don't see   631

When the sight leaves the eye, love leaves the heart   632

After the settlement (the dowry) comes the love   633

Love is blind to blemishes and faults   634

Love hides ignominy and evil   635

Love is no impartial judge   636

House without hound, cat, or child, house without
    love or affection   637

Love a woman or a child without their knowing it   638

To the raven her own chick is white   639

What is nearest the heart is usually nearest the lips   640

What is nearest the heart comes out   641

Love cools quickly   642

Love conceals ugliness, and hate sees a lot of faults   643

She who fills the heart fills the eye   644

There's no love until there's a family   645

Absence makes the heart grow fond   646

LUCK

It's better to be lucky than to be an early riser   647

A chance shot will not kill the Devil   648

The man who has luck in the morning has luck in the
    afternoon   649

There's luck in sharing   650

It's better to be lucky than wise   651

A meeting in the sunlight is lucky, and a burying in
    the rain   652

The lucky person has only to be born   653

Luck seldom lasts   654

MANNERS

Without store no friends; without rearing no manners   655

Better good manners than good looks   656

MARRIAGE

The husband of the sloven is known in the field amidst
a crowd   657

A growing moon and a flowing tide are lucky times
to marry in   658

Never make a toil of pleasure, as the man said when he
dug his wife's grave only three feet deep   659

Marriage at the dungheap and the godparents far away   660

Woe to him who does not heed a good wife's counsel   661

It's why women marry … the creatures, God bless
them, are too shy to say no   662

There was never an old slipper but there was an old
stocking to match it   663

A young man is bothered till he's married; after that
he's bothered entirely   664

There's only one thing in the world better than a good
wife … no wife   665

The dowry falls over the cliff; but the protruding lip
remains on the wife   666

A bad wife takes advice from everyone but her husband   667

He breaks his wife's head and then buys a plaster for it   668

There are no trials till marriage   669

The carefree mother's daughter makes a bad wife   670

It's a lonesome washing that there's not a (man's) shirt in   671

Marry a mountainy woman and you'll marry the
mountain   672

She's a good woman, but she didn't take off her boots yet   673

The day you marry your wife you marry your children   674

The blanket is the warmer of being doubled   675

She burnt her coal and did not warm herself   676

He married money and got a woman with it   677

Marry in haste and be sorry at your leisure   678

MATURITY

By age or ability you're no child   679

MEANNESS

What you give wouldn't blind the eye of a midge   680

As tight as tuppence in a market-woman's trashbag   681

If you give the loan of your britches, don't cut off the
buttons   682

'Tis strange that the man who is so quick
to find fault is himself so stingy about food   683

To come with one hand longer than the other   684

Nothing comes into a closed hand   685

MEN

Some men are like bagpipes … they can't speak till
   their bellies are filled   686

MISFORTUNE

From the house of the Devil to the house of the demon   687

After misfortune the Irishman sees his profit   688

It is well that misfortunes come one by one and not
   all together   689

It's easy to sleep on the misfortune of others   690

When misfortune is greatest relief is nearest   681

There's worse than this in the North   692

Nothing is ever as bad as it seems   693

The old white horse is the end of all misfortune   694

Speak to misfortune when it comes   695

No heightening the grief of a sorrowful man   696

MOTHER

He is scant of news that speaks ill of his mother   697

A busy mother makes a lazy daughter   698

A mother with a pouch is better than a father with a
   ploughteam   699

NATURE

You won't get from a cat but its skin   700

The lamb is a sheep in the long run   701

Its nature breaks out through the eyes of the cat   702

Let the tail go with the hide   703

A wild goose never laid a tame egg   704

What can you expect from a pig but a grunt   705

How could the apple be but like the apple tree   706

Nature is stronger than nurture   707

He got it from nature as the pig got the rooting in the
    ground   708

Often a cow does not take after its breed   709

What would a young cat do but eat mice?   710

Nature will come through the claws, and the hound
    will follow the hare   711

If you put a silk dress on a goat he is a goat still   712

Every bird as it is reared and the lark for the bog   713

What is in the marrow is hard to take out of the bone   714

The wood will renew the foliage it sheds   715

What will come from the briar but the berry   716

The hand goes only where the leg goes   717

NEATNESS

A handstaff of holly, a *buailtín* of hazel, a single sheaf
and a clean floor (*see notes*)   718

NECESSITY

One who is without cows must be his own dog   719

Make necessity a virtue   720

Necessity accepts no law   721

A blind man can see his mouth   722

You never miss the water till the well has run dry   723

NOBILITY

A king's son is not nobler than his food   724

OBEDIENCE

Keep your tongue in your jaw and your toe in your
pump   725

OBLIGATION

Pity the man who has a stranger's spancel on him   726

OWNERSHIP

To every cow its calf; to every book its copy (*see notes*)   727

PARTICIPATION

Watching is a part of good play 728

PATIENCE

By degrees the castles are built 729

When the apple is ripe, it will fall 730

Patience cures many an old complaint 731

The one who waits the fine day will get the fine day 732

Patience and forbearance made a bishop of his
reverence 733

Patience can conquer destiny 734

Patience is a plaster for all sores 735

For what cannot be cured patience is best 736

There is not a tree in Heaven higher than the tree of
patience 737

Patience is a virtue that causes no shame 738

Time and patience would bring the snail to Jerusalem 739

PATRIOTISM

Everyone praises his native land 740

PEACE

Nobody ever bought peace but the man who hadn't
got it 741

Peace (quietness) is worth buying   742

The world's quiet and the pig is in the sty   743

Least said soonest mended   744

No matter who succeeds or fails, the peacemaker will
always suffer   745

To the fighting man peace is sure   746

The end of a feast is better than the beginning of a
fight   747

PERCEPTION

An eye is blind in another man's corner   748

One eye in the corner is sharper than two about
the house   749

PITY

He's more to be pitied than laughed at   750

Don't tell your complaint to one who has no pity   751

POETRY

A poem ought to be well made at first, for there is
many a one to spoil it afterwards   752

POSSESSION

It's better than it's want   753

Have it yourself, or else do without it   754

Better the certainty of the straddle (packsaddle) than
    the mere loan of a saddle   755

Possession is nine-tenths of the law   756

Better own a trifle than want a great deal   757

A wren in the hand is better than a crane to be caught   758

Possession satisfies   759

A bird in the hand is worth two in the bush   760

It's better than the loan you couldn't get   761

Half a loaf is better than no bread   762

A live dog is better than a dead lion   763

A trout in the pot is better than a salmon in the sea   764

POVERTY

Put a beggar on horseback and he'll ride to Hell   765

Put a beggar on horseback and he'll go on a gallop   766

Poverty parts good company   767

Poverty destroys companionship   768

Many a defect is seen in the poor man   769

It's hard to take britches off bare hips   770

The full man does not understand the wants of the
    hungry   771

A little pleases a poor man   772

Poor men take to the sea; the rich to the mountains   773

Poverty creates sadness   774

Pity the man who does wrong and is poor as well	775
There is nothing in the world so poor as going to Hell	776
The thief is no danger to the beggar	777
Poverty is no shame	778
Two things that go to loss: turf on a mountain and the wisdom of a poor man	779
Shame is ever a part of poverty	780
No one is ever poor who has the sight of his eyes and the use of his feet	781
There is no tune without a penny	782
A poor man never yet lost his property	783
Poor is the church without music	784
A smokey cabin, a handful of spuds and a flea-filled bed	785

POWER

No stopping the force of a going wheel by hand	786
No forcing the sea	787

PRESUMPTION

Don't count your chickens before they are hatched	788
Don't bless the fish till it gets to the land	789
Don't build the sty until the litter comes	790
Praise the ripe field not the green corn	791
Praise the ford when you have crossed it	792

You must empty a box before you fill it again 793

PRIDE

The pride of women and the pride of priests 794

It is difficult to soothe the proud 795

Pride comes before a fall 796

Pride feels no pain 797

Pride is the author of every sin 798

The jump of a cock on the dungheap 799

PROCRASTINATION

There is no virtue in the herb that is not got in time 800

A postponement till morning, a postponement for
ever 801

It is no time to go for the doctor when the patient is
dead 802

PROMISE

A promise is a debt 803

PROVERBS

Proverbs cannot be contradicted 804

The proverb cannot be bettered 805

Though the proverb is abandoned, it is not falsified 806

PRUDENCE

Don't throw out the dirty water until you have the
   clean water in   807

It's better to return from the centre of the ford than
   drown in the flood   808

The sty before the litter   809

RED HAIR

If you meet a red-haired woman, you'll meet a crowd   810

To be red-haired is better than to be without a head   811

REPENTANCE

To put off repentance is dangerous   812

It's better to be sorry and stay than to be sorry and
   go away   813

REPUTATION

It's a small thing that outlives a man   814

Remember even if you lose all, keep your good name,
   for if you lose that you are worthless   815

Those who get the name of rising early may lie all day   816

When a man gets his feet in the lime he cannot easily
   get rid of it   817

REVENGE

No dealing with a revengeful man   818

ROGUE

He was never good since the time a yard (of cloth)
    made a coat for him   819

Don't mention him and a decent man in the one day   820

A sly rogue is often in good dress   821

She would drink the cream and say the cat she had was
    an old rogue   822

The horse with the most scars is the one that highest
    kicks his rear   823

RUMOUR

The person who brings a story to you will take away
    two from you   824

A story without an author is not worth listening to 825

Leave the bad tale where you found it   826

There is no smoke without fire   827

SCARCITY

When all fruits fail, welcome haws   828

When the fruit is scarcest, its taste is sweetest   829

We have a fine day more often than a kiln-cast   830

SEASONS

A soft-dropping April brings milk to cows and sheep   831

Autumn days come quickly like the running of a
    hound on the moor   832

A misty winter brings a pleasant spring, a pleasant
    winter a misty spring   833

Many a sudden change takes place on a spring day   834

In winter the milk goes to the cow's horns   835

SECRET

A secret is a weapon and a friend   836

It is no secret that is known to three   837

Fences (ditches) have ears   838

Don't tell your secret even to a fence   839

Woe to the man that entrusts his secrets to a ditch   840

The secret of an old woman scolding   841

If it's a secret, it's binding   842

Don't tell secrets to the children of your relatives   843

SELF-DESTRUCTION

No tree but has rotten wood enough to burn it   844

A man may be his own ruin   845

A wedge from itself splits the oak tree   846

A man has often cut a rod to beat himself   847

selfishness

It's for her own good that the cat purrs 848

His own wound is what everyone feels soonest 849

What is nearest the heart is nearest the mouth 850

He who is best to me is he who shall get the best share 851

The full stomach does not understand the empty one 852

The man who was dividing Ireland didn't leave himself
last 853

sense

Sense doesn't come before age 854

separation

After the gathering comes the scattering 855

shame

What would shame him would turn back a funeral 856

A fist full of gain and a village full of shame 857

Better is the trouble that follows death than the trouble
that follows shame 858

shyness

Do not keep your tongue under your belt 859

A man is shy in another man's corner   860

SILENCE

A silent mouth is musical   861

The silent are often guilty   862

The silent mouth is sweet to hear   863

When wrathful words arise, a closed mouth is soothing   864

The stars make no noise   865

Little talk is easy to cure   866

A closed mouth ... a wise head   867

A silent mouth never did any harm   868

STRENGTH

Strength is not enduring   869

STUPIDITY

Sending the goose on a message to the fox's den   870

Putting the fox to mind the geese   871

You didn't turn up when sense was being distributed   872

SUCCESS

There's neither success nor efficiency without authority
    and laws   873

Fat is not to be had without labour   874

SUITABILITY

The windy day is not the day for thatching   875

One's man meat is another man's poison   876

Whoever the cap fits takes it   877

TACT

Better sit beside him than in his place   878

A short visit is best and that not too often   879

The eye should be blind in the home of another   880

It's often a man's mouth broke his nose   881

Don't say everything you want to say lest you hear
    something you would not like to hear   882

Don't let your tongue cut your throat   883

See not what you see and hear not what you hear   884

Never speak to the feet while the head is alive   885

Don't rest your eyes beyond what is your own   886

It's bad manners to talk about ropes in the house
    of a man whose father was hanged   887

TALENT

A greyhound finds food in its feet   888

The slow hound often has good qualities   889

The bird that can sing and won't sing should be made
    to sing   890

A cat between two houses, a rabbit between two holes,
the two liveliest   891

TALKATIVENESS

Great talk and little action   892

Do not be talkative in an alehouse   893

You kissed the blarney stone   894

THRIFT

A spender gets the property of the hoarder   895

Let your bargain suit your purpose   896

Spread your cloth only as you can draw it   897

TIME

The waiting man thinks the time long   898

A watched kettle never boils   899

Time is a good storyteller   900

TREACHERY

He who spies is the one who kills   901

Treachery returns   902

TROUBLE

There's trouble in every house and some in the street   903

Everything troubles you and the cat breaks your heart 904

TRUST

The fox never found a better messenger than himself 905

Never trust a spiteful man 906

TRUTH

A man with a loud laugh makes truth itself seem folly 907

Truth is great and will win out 908

Even the truth may be bitter 909

There are two tellings to every story 910

Drunkenness and anger 'tis said tell the truth 911

What I'm afraid to hear I'd better say first myself 912

Truth speaks even though the tongue were dead 913

You can keep away from the rogue, but you cannot
keep yourself safe from the liar 914

Truth stands when everything else falls 915

It is no shame to tell the truth 916

Tell the truth and shame the Devil 917

UNDERSTANDING

The well-filled belly has little understanding of the
empty 918

'Tis afterwards that everything is understood 919

USELESSNESS

It's a bad hound that's not worth the whistling   920

He knows how many grains to a bushel of wheat   921

He knows the price of everything and the value
  of nothing   922

He couldn't drag a herring off the coals   923

It's just a wisp in place of a brush   924

VALUE

One pair of good soles is worth two pairs of upper
  leathers   925

Without pressing too little or too hard, hold tight the
  reins for he's a fool who would not get value from
  a borrowed horse   926

It's not worth a cuckoo-spit   927

Better an idle house than a bad tenant   928

VANITY

Pity him who makes his opinion a certainty   929

He thinks that he himself is the very stone that was
  hurled at the castle   930

He dotes on his midden and thinks it the moon   931

WARNING

That's a spoon ye'll sup sorrow with yet   932

WASTEFULNESS

Wilful waste makes woeful want   933

WEALTH

A shamefaced man seldom acquires wealth   934

The money-maker (profiteer) is never tired   935

The doorstep of a great house is slippery   936

There is misfortune only where there is wealth   937

Sweet is the voice of the man who has wealth   938

A hut is a palace to a poor man   939

A heavy purse makes a light heart   940

There's little value in the single cow   941

A man of one cow – a man of no cow   942

It's easy to knead when meal is at hand   943

WEATHER

Wind from the east is good for neither man nor beast   944

A Kerry shower is of twenty-four hours   945

Better April showers than the breadth of the ocean in
   gold   946

WELCOME

Better for a man to have even a dog welcome him
than a dog bark at him   947

Going in is not the same as going out   948

A welcome is a debtor's face   949

WIDOW

What's all the world to a man when his wife is a widow   950

WISDOM

A wise head keeps a shut mouth   951

Everyone is wise till he speaks   952

Food is no more important than wisdom   953

A contraction (in writing) is enough for a scholar   954

The beginning of wisdom is the fear of God   955

There's no wise man without a fault   956

He may die of wind but he'll never die of wisdom   957

You can't put a wise head on young shoulders   958

Wisdom is what makes a poor man a king,
a weak person powerful, a good generation
of a bad one, a foolish man reasonable   959

Though wisdom is good in the beginning, it is better
at the end   960

A little of anything isn't worth a pin, but a wee bit of
sense is worth a lot   961

No making of a wise man   962

WOMEN

A dishonest woman can't be kept in, and an honest
   woman won't   963

There is no thing wickeder than a woman of evil temper   964

A bad woman (/wife) drinks a lot of her own bad
   butter-milk   965

A foolish woman knows a foolish man's faults   966

A whistling woman and a crowing hen will bring no
   luck to the house they are in   967

Beef to the heels like a Mullingar heifer   968

Eight lives for the men and nine for the women   969

Wherever there are women there's talking, and
   wherever there's geese there's cackling   970

Irishwomen have a dispensation from the Pope to
   wear the thick ends of their legs downwards   971

Women are shy and shame prevents them from
   refusing a man   972

Everything dear is a woman's fancy   973

Like an Irish wolf she barks at her own shadow   974

She wipes the plate with the cat's tail   975

More hair than tit, like a mountain heifer   976

Women are stronger than men, they do not die of
   wisdom   977

When the old woman is hard pressed, she has to run   978

It's difficult to trust a woman	979
Man to the hills, woman to the shore	980
Beat a woman with a hammer and you'll have gold	981
'Tis as hard to see a woman cry as a goose go barefoot	982
'Where comes a cow', the wise man [St Colmcille] lay down, 'there follows a woman, and where comes a woman follows trouble'	983
Only a fool would prefer food to a woman	984
Don't be ever in court or a castle without a woman to make your excuse	985
An excuse is nearer to a woman than her apron	986
There is nothing sharper than a woman's tongue	987
A woman without is she who has neither pipe nor child	988
The yellow *praiseach* (kale) of the fields that brings the Meath women to harm	989
A woman like a goose, a sharp pecking woman A woman like a pig, a sleepy-headed woman A woman like a sickle, a strong stubborn woman A woman like a goat, a woman of rushing visits A woman like a sheep, an affable friendly woman A woman like a lamb, a quiet friendly woman	990
It is not the most beautiful woman who has the most sense	991
A woman can beat the Devil	992
A shrew gets her wish but suffers in the getting	993

WORK

Many a time, the man with ten (cows) has overtaken
the man with forty (cows)   994

Do it as if there were fire in your skin   995

The seeking for one thing will find another   996

Make your hay before the fine weather leaves you   997

Sow early and mow early   998

The early riser gets through his business but not
through early rising   999

The slow horse reaches the mill   1000

Making the beginning is one third of the work   1001

The quiet pigs eat all the draff   1002

The sweat of one's brow is what burns everyone   1003

Everyone lays a burden on the willing horse   1004

Every little makes a mickle   1005

Speed and accuracy do not agree   1006

Never put off tomorrow what you can do today   1007

I'll go there tonight for evening is speedier than
morning   1008

The person of the greatest talk is the person of the
least work   1009

Be there with the day and be gone with the day   1010

About evening a man is known   1011

Long churning makes bad butter   1012

Scattering is easier than gathering	1013
The labour of the crow	1014
Put it on your shoulder and say it is not a burden	1015
It's no delay to stop to edge the tool	1016
The mason who strikes often is better than the one who strikes too hard	1017
It destroys the craft not to learn it	1018
The dog that's always on the go is better than the one that's always curled up	1019
Handfuls make a load	1020
Don't go early or late to the well	1021
A good beginning is half the work	1022

YOUTh

Praise the young and they will make progress	1023
Many a shabby colt makes a fine horse	1024
The young shed many skins	1025
Youth likes to wander	1026
The growth of the gosling	1027
Youth cannot believe	1028

 TRIADS

Three As Good As

Three things as good as the best: dirty water to quench
a fire, a frieze coat on a frosty day and black bread
in famine time   1029

Three things that are as good as things better than
them: a wooden sword in a coward's hand, an ugly
wife married to a blind man and poor clothes on
a drunken man   1030

Three Best

Three best friends and three worst enemies: fire, wind
and rain   1031

Three best to have in plenty: sunshine, wisdom and
generosity   1032

Three best things to have a surplus of: money after
paying the rent, seed after spring and friends at
home   1033

Three best invitations: come to mass, come and make
secure and come to the mill   1034

Three with best sight: the eye of a blacksmith on a nail,
the eye of a young girl at a contest and the eye of a
priest on his parish   1035

Three best small: a beehive, a sheep and a woman   1036

The three best sounds: the sound of the flail,
the sound of the quern, the sound of the churn   1037

THREE FORTUNES

The three fortunes of the cat: the housewife's
forgetfulness, walking without a sound and
keen sight in darkness   1038

Three fortunes of the lucky man: fences, vigilance
and early rising   1039

Three fortunes of the unlucky man: long visits to his
neighbours, long morning sleep and bad fences   1040

THREE HARDEST

The three hardest to go through: a waterfall, a bog
and a briary track   1041

The three hardest to select: a Sunday woman, an
autumn sheep and an old mare's foal   1042

THREE KINDS

The three kinds of brain: brain as hard as stone, brain
as receptive as wax and brain as unstable as flowing
water   1043

The three kinds of men: the worker, the pleasure-seeker
and the boaster   1044

The three kinds of men who fail to understand women:
young men, old men and middle-aged men   1045

The three kinds of men who rise earliest: the husband
of a talkative wife, the man with a stolen white
horse and the man with the dirty tattered shirt   1046

The three kinds of poor people: the man poor
by the will of God, the man poor by his own will
and the man poor even if he owned the world   1047

The three kinds of women: the woman as
shameless as a pig, the woman as unruly as a hen
and the woman as gentle as a lamb   1048

Three Most

Three most bothersome things in the world: a thorn
in the foot, a woman and a goat going to the fair
that will go any way but the way you want it   1049

The three most delightful things to see: a garden
of white potatoes covered in blossom,
a ship under sail and a woman after giving birth   1050

The three most difficult to select: a woman, a scythe
and a razor   1051

The three most difficult to teach: a mule, a pig and a
woman   1052

The three most difficult to understand: the mind of a
woman, the labour of the bees and the ebb and flow
of the tide   1053

The three most fortunate things a man ever had:
a mare, a sow and a goose   1054

The three most nourishing foods: beef marrow,
the flesh of a chicken, Scandinavian beer   1055

The three most pleasant things: a cat's kitten,
a goat's kid and a young widow-woman   1056

The three most troubled eyes: the eye of a blacksmith
after the nail, the eye of a chicken after the grain
and the eye of a girl seeking her sweetheart   1057

ThREE TRAITS

Three traits of a bull: a bold walk, a strong neck
and a hard forehead   1058

Three traits of a fox: a light step, a look to the front
and a glance to each side of the road   1059

Three traits of a hare: a lively ear, a bright eye
and a quick run against the hill   1060

Three traits of a woman: a broad bosom,
a slender waist and a short back   1061

ThREE UGLIEST

The three ugliest things that are: a hairless mangy dog,
a woman without flesh or blood and a deceitful,
shameless girl   1062

The three ugliest things of their own kind: a thin
red-haired woman, a thin yellow horse and a
thin white cow   1063

ThREE USELESS

The three things useless when old: an old schoolmaster,
an old horse and an old soldier   1064

Three things that are of little use: a trumpet and no
tongue, a button and no buttonhole and a wolf
without teeth   1065

Three Worst

The three worst departures: leaving mass before it
ends, leaving table without grace and
leaving your wife to go to another woman   1066

The three worst endings: the last days of a noble old
lady, the last days of an old white horse and the last
days of an old schoolmaster   1067

The three worst endings: a house burning, a ship
sinking and an old white horse dying   1068

The three worst pets: a pet priest, a pet beggar
and a pet pig   1069

The three worst things to have in a house: a scolding
wife, a smokey chimney and a leaky roof   1070

The three worse things of all: small, soft potatoes, from
that to an uncomfortable bed and to sleep with
a bad woman   1071

Three Things

The things that cannot be acquired: voice, generosity
and poetry   1072

Three things that arrive unnoticed: rent, age and
a beard   1073

Three things to beware of: the hoof of the horse,
the horn of the bull and the smile of the Saxon
(*see notes*)   1074

Three things a man should not boast of: the size of his
purse, the beauty of his wife and the sweetness of
his beer   1075

Three things bright at first, then dull and finally black: co-operation, a marriage alliance and living in the one house   1076

Three things Christ never intended: a woman whistling, a hound howling and a hen crowing   1077

Three things that relate to drink: to pay for it, to drink it and to carry it   1078

Three things that fill a haggard: ambition, industry and constant vigilance   1079

Three good things to have: a clean shirt, a clean conscience and a guinea in the pocket   1080

Three disagreeable things at home: a scolding wife, a squalling child and a smoky chimney   1081

Three things that don't bear nursing: an old woman, a hen and a sheep   1082

Three things that are purposeless: throwing a stone on a bend, giving advice to a wrathful woman, talking to a head without sense   1083

Three things that remain longest in a family: fighting, red hair and thieving   1084

Three things that don't remain: a white cow, a handsome woman and a house on a height   1085

Three things that can never return: a Sunday without mass, a day away from school and a day away from work   1086

Three things that won't have rest: a steep waterfall, an otter and a devil out of Hell   1087

Three things that never rust: a woman's tongue, the shoes of a butcher's horse and charitable people's money   1088

Three things that never rust: a sword, a spade and a thought   1089

Three things never seen: a blade's edge, wind and love 1090

Three sharpest things that are: a hound's tooth, a thorn in the mud and a fool's word   1091

The three sharpest things: a fool's word, a thorn in the mud and a soft woollen thread that cuts to the bone   1092

Three things that survive for the shortest time: a woman's association, the love of a mare for her foal and fresh oaten bread   1093

Three thing swiftest in the sea: the seal, the ray and the mackerel   1094

Three things swiftest on land: the hound, the hare and the fox   1095

Three things that leave the shortest traces: a bird on a branch, a ship on the sea and a man on a woman   1096

Three things that leave the longest traces: charcoal on wood, a chisel on a block of stone and a ploughshare on a furrow   1097

Three things not to be trusted: a fine day in winter, the life of an old person or the word of an important man unless it's in writing   1098

Three things not be trusted: a cow's horn, a dog's
tooth and a horse's hoof   1099

Three things of least value in any house: too many
geese in a house without a lake, too many women
in a house without wool to be spun, too many
horses in a house without ploughing to be done   1100

Three things that have little value: the head of a
woodcock, the head of a goat and the head of
a gurnet   1101

Three things a man should not be without: a cat, a
chimney and a housewife   1102

MISCELLANEOUS

Three parts of the body most easily hurt: the knee, the
elbow and the eye   1103

Three that do not clean their snouts: the farmer, the
dog and the pig   1104

Three coldest things that are: a hound's snout, a man's
knee and a woman's breast   1105

Three to whom it's little sense to pay a compliment:
an old man, a bad man and a child   1106

Three deaths that ought not be bemoaned: the death
of a fat hog, the death of a thief and the death of
a proud prince   1107

Three the Devil has without much trouble: the
mason, the bailiff and the miller   1108

Three enemies of the body: wind, smoke and fleas   1109

Three errors relating to corn: to cut it green, to grind it damp and to eat it fresh 1110

Three great evils: smallness of house, closeness of heart and shortage of food 1111

Three with the sharpest eyes: a hawk on a tree, a fox in a glen, a young girl at a meeting 1112

Three wholesome foods for the driver: the back of a herring, the belly of a salmon and the head of a thrush (/moorhen) 1113

Three bad habits: drinking the glass, smoking the pipe and scattering the dew late at night 1114

Three happiest in the world: the tailor, the piper and the goat 1115

Three strokes that are keeping Ireland: the stroke of an axe on a block, of a hammer on an anvil and of a threshing flail in the centre 1116

Three jobs that must be done with vigour: rowing, hammering and measuring the ground with your fist (i.e. using the sickle) 1117

Three kind acts unrequited: that done for an old man, for a wicked person or for a little child 1118

Three sweetest melodies: the churning of butter, the plough ploughing and the mill grinding 1119

Three oaths that money swore: that it did not care who would possess it, that it would stay but a while with any man and that it would not stay with any man but the man who loved it 1120

Three pair that never agree: two married women
in the same house, two cats with one mouse
and two bachelors after the one young woman 1121

Three places that cannot be avoided: the place
of birth, the place of death and the place of burial 1122

Three times it is most likely to rain: early on Friday,
late on Saturday and on Sunday morning when
it's time for first mass 1123

Three greatest rushes: the rush of water, the rush of
fire and the rush of falsehood 1124

Three sauciest by nature: a ram, a bull and a tailor 1125

Three skills of the hare: sharp turning, high jumping
and strong running against the hill 1126

Three strongest forces: the force of fire, the force of
water and the force of hatred 1127

Three truths: sunrise, sunset and death 1128

Three unluckiest things to meet first thing in the
morning: a mad dog, a man who lent you money
and a red-haired girl 1129

Three virtues of the drunkard: a miserable morning,
a dirty coat and an empty pocket 1130

Three signs of an unfortunate man: going bail,
intervening in disputes and giving evidence 1131

The three characteristics of the Fianna: purity of heart,
strength of limb and acting according to our word 1132

FOURSOMES

Four priests who are not greedy; four Frenchmen
who are not yellow (cowardly); four cobblers who
don't tell lies; that's twelve not in this country   1133

Four things an Irishman should not trust: a cow's
horn, a horse's hoof, a dog's snarl and an
Englishman's laugh (*compare no. 1074*)   1134

The four fortunes of the cat: the housewife's error,
walking without care, no water in milk and sight
at night as well as by day (*compare no. 1038*)   1135

Four hateful things: a worthless hound, a slow horse,
a chief without wisdom and a wife without
children   1136

NOTES

Proverb 51

The *buailtín* is the Irish word for the part of the flail that strikes the corn.

Proverb 52

Ciotóg is the Irish word for a left-handed person; it often implies awkwardness. In this instance, however, the implication is one of the cuteness or guile. Various superstitions have been associated with the *ciotóg* – including suspicion of evil or treachery (note the English word 'sinister', from the Latin).

Proverb 56

The Irish word *meitheal* means a team of workers (neighbours) assisting one another at turf-cutting or hay-making. The blacksmith usually had the largest *meitheal* in the parish since his work at the forge was of such importance to the community.

Proverb 61

'The Old Woman of Beare': a legendary figure in Irish folklore and poetry. (See Patrick Pearse's poem, 'Mise Eire' and Austin Clarke's 'The Young Woman of Beare'.)

Proverb 72

About AD 300, when Cormac mac Airt was High King of Ireland, ruling from Tara, a warrior army called the Fianna was formed under the leadership of Fionn mac Cumhaill. Around the Fianna and its leader grew a great body of legend still popular today. Fionn himself was noted for his bravery and wisdom (he tasted the salmon of knowledge). The Fianna eventually became too powerful for the High King but were defeated at the battle of Gabhra and disbanded.

Proverb 208

The word 'cess', according to P. W. Joyce, may mean a contraction of success, or a 'contribution'. He refers to its use in County Louth as meaning a quantity of corn in for threshing.

Proverb 279

Lough Sheelin is a large lake in County Cavan.

Proverb 451

Used as a reply when you are reminded by someone of a favour they have granted you.

Proverb 606 and 609

'Speckled' refers to the 'heat-spots' got on the shins from sitting too long and too close by the fire.

Proverb 718

For *buailtín*, see note under proverb 51 above.

Proverb 727

This proverb is King Diarmuid's famous judgement, given about AD 560, on the ownership of a manuscript copy made by St Colmcille of a manuscript belonging to St Finnian. It must be one of our first copyright laws.

Proverb 1074

Another shorter, blunt saying affirms the fear and mistrust of the occupying English colonists: 'Beware the Sassanach.'

INDEX

ability 1–7, 679
absence 400, 646
accuracy 1006
achievement 262
acknowledge 154
acquire (to) 1072
act 308, 1118, 1132
action 892
address (to) 430
advice 8–14, 667, 1083
affectation 15–18
affection 637
afraid 348, 349
afternoon 649
age 19–27, 679, 854, 1073
agree (to) 1006, 1121
ale 477
alehouse 893
alive 885
alliance 1076
allot 468
alms 152, 160
alone 421
amadán 375, 377
ambition 1079
angel 18
anger 28–31, 453, 911
answer 453
anvil 1116
apart 594

appear 185
appearance 32–8
apple 706, 730
apple-tree 706
apply (to) 603
April 831, 946
apron 986
arm 170
army 563
arrive (to) 1073
art 39
as … as 40–81
ashes 26, 30
ass 203
attack (to) 563
author 798, 825
authority 873
autumn 609, 832, 1042
avoid (to) 1122
axe 1116
bachelors 1121
back 232, 261, 264, 532, 1061
backside 607
bad 44, 95, 106, 149, 172, 207–8, 311, 314–15, 693, 826, 887, 920, 928, 965, 1012, 1071, 1114
bag 436
bagpipes 686

bail 1131
bailiff 1108
bald 51
ball 566
baptise (to) 165
barb 244
bard 31
bare 172, 607
barefoot 982
bargain 896
bark 357
bark (to) 3, 430, 595, 947, 974
Barrington 44
bashful 69
beak 302
beard 1073
beast 944
beat (to) 300, 847
beautiful 33, 86
beauty 83–7, 161, 1075
bed 785, 1071
bee 76, 1053
beef 968, 1055
beehive 1036
beer 1055, 1075
beetle 588
beggar 160, 765–6, 777, 1069
beg (to) 150, 445
beget (to) 283, 312, 475

beginning 504, 513, 747

believe (to) 1028

belly 187, 446, 546, 686, 918, 1113

belt 859

bend (to) 188

berry 55, 716

best 1031–7

betray 88

beware (to) 112, 124, 1074

big 56

binding 842

bird 22, 322, 616, 713, 760, 890, 1096

birth 1050, 1122

bishop 733

bite (to) 122

bitter 53, 161, 271, 395, 909

bitterness 89

black 37, 43, 82, 147, 1076

blackguard 258

blacksmith 1035, 1057

blade 1090

blame 313, 368

blanket 675

Blarney 894

blemish 634

bless (to) 662, 789

blessing 90–100, 551

blind 174, 305, 390, 433, 595–6, 634, 680, 722, 748, 880, 1030

block 1097, 1116

blood 355, 392, 396, 438, 589, 1062

bloodhound 44

blossom 1050

blow 29, 354, 388, 603

board 504

boast (to) 101, 154–5, 1075

boaster 1044

body 1103, 1109

bog 125, 713, 1041

bold 110

bond 585

bone 33, 114, 187, 298, 354, 484, 714, 1092

book 287, 502, 596, 727

boot 673

born 338, 653

borrow (to) 102–6, 926

bosom 1061

bothered (to be) 664

bothersome 1049

box 793

brain 1043

branch 1096

bravery 72, 107–10

bread 482, 762, 1029, 1093

break (to) 270, 298, 343, 454, 602, 668

breast 1105

breath 432

breed 709

breed (to) 335

briar 488, 716, 1041

bribery 111–14, 238

bright 63

britches 682, 770

brood 630

broom 146

broth 123

brother 229, 426

brow 1003

brown 55

brush 924

buailtín 51, 718

buckle 38

build (to) 729

bull 1058, 1074, 1125

burden 29, 289, 467, 610, 1004, 1015

burn (to) 190, 316, 324, 378, 449, 587, 676, 844, 1003, 1068

bury (to) 652, 1122

bush 437, 493, 760

bushel 921

business 586, 999

busy 76, 698

butcher 1088

butter 511, 1119

butter (to) 358

buttermilk 483, 965

button 682

buy (to) 325, 404, 668, 741, 742

cabin 785

Cailleach Beare 61

calf 100, 249, 727

candle 449

cane 261

cap 877

card-player 443

care 136, 1135

carefree 670

carelessness 115–17

castle 729, 930, 985

cat 26, 301, 324, 350,
    487, 637, 700, 702,
    710, 822, 848, 891,
    904, 975, 1038,
    1056, 1102, 1121,
    1135

catch (to) 117, 130, 233,
    294–5, 322, 539

cattle 117, 379

caution 118–44

cease (to) 396, 423

certainty 929

chafer 590

chaff 322

chance 648

change 145–7

character 148

characteristics 1132

charcoal 1097

charitable 1088

charity 149–60

chastity 161

cheek 392

cherries 8

chicken 639, 788, 1055,
    1057

chief 31, 618

children 98, 162–71,
    179, 316, 561,
    637–8, 674, 679,
    843, 988, 1081,
    1105, 1118, 1136

chimney 1070, 1081,
    1102

chisel 1097

choice 172–4, 370

Christ 1077

church 784

churchyard 228

churn 487, 1037

churning 1012, 1119

ciotóg 52

claws 711

clay 221

clean (to) 1104

clergy, *see also* bishop;
    nun; priest 175–84

cliff 220, 666

clock 619

cloth 819, 897

clothes 15, 1030

clown 370

coal 378, 676, 923

coat 351, 819, 1029,
    1130

cobbler 1133

cock 22, 799

coffin 513

coincidence 185

cold 210, 606

coldness 419

colour 429

colt 1024

comb 236, 515

comfort 186–7

companion 219

company 409, 421,
    767–8

complain (to) 492

complaint 731, 751

compliment 1106

compromise 188

comrade 399

conflict 10

confusion 289

conquer (to) 255, 734

conscience 1080

contempt 335

contentment 189–90

continue (to) 618

contraction 954

contradict (to) 804

conversation 191–3

cook (to) 413

cool (to) 642

co-operation 1076

copy 727

corn 543, 791, 1110

corner 748, 749, 860

cottage 448

cough 513

counsel 661

count (to) 788

countenance 147

country 427, 1133

court (to) 411, 599,

601, 985
courtship 194–5
cover (to) 417
covetous 489, 490
cow 220, 251, 360, 709,
    719, 727, 831, 835,
    941–2, 983, 994,
    1063, 1085, 1099,
    1134
coward 1030
cowardly 1133
craft 1018
crane 204, 758
cravat 170
cream 822
creature 662
criticism 196–8
Cromwell 214
crooked 54, 261
cross 203, 792
crow 1014
crow (to) 1077
crowd 110, 657, 810
crown 491
cry (to) 163, 375, 545,
    982
cuckoo-spit 927
cunning 48, 199–205
curds 173
cure 224, 276, 499, 502,
    510, 511, 518
cure (to) 382, 731, 736,
    866
curse 206–14
cut (to) 883

cut off (to) 682
cynicism 215–16
daisy 62
Damer 79
damp 1110
dance 21
danger 217–20, 348,
    777, 812
dark 256, 341, 422,
    1038
daughter 171, 670, 698
dawn 341
day 210, 221, 337, 344,
    541, 612, 732, 816,
    830, 875, 1010,
    1067, 1098, 1135
dead 330, 360, 432,
    802, 913
death 207, 212, 221–41,
    356, 382, 478, 611,
    858, 1107, 1122,
    1128
debt 242–3, 457, 803,
    949
decay 23
decent 820
deception 244–50
decline (to) 627
deed 154, 155, 157, 311
deep 68, 84, 248, 659
deer 5
defect 769
delay 1016
delightful 1050
delusion 251–4

demon 687
den 870
departure 1066
desire 255
despair 256
destiny 734
destroy (to) 267, 1018
Devil 18, 185, 257–60,
    441, 599, 648, 687,
    917, 992, 1087, 1108
dew 515, 1114
die (to) 91, 225, 977,
    1068
difficult 174, 1051–3
dig (to) 659
dinner 64
directs 463
dirty 351, 616
disagree (to) 397
discipline 261–3
disease 277, 505
dish 577
dishonour 23
dismissal 264
dispensation 971
disposition 166
dispute 578, 1131
distant 180
ditch 197, 838–9
doctor 502, 510, 802
dog 21, 42, 108, 114,
    129, 268, 351, 420,
    430, 484, 536, 595,
    719, 761, 947, 1019,
    1062, 1099, 1104,

1129, 1134
Donal 278
donkey 74
door 108, 455, 459
doorstep 936
dote (to) 931
dour 422
dowry 633, 666
draff 1002
drag (to) 923
dram 280
dress 712, 821
drink 265–284, 394, 1078, 1114
drinker 444
drive (to) 437
driver 1113
drop 267
drown (to) 135, 340, 808
drunk 31, 266, 282, 441
drunkard 1130
drunken 1030
drunkenness 911
druid 31
dry 226, 279, 723
dull 65, 1076
dumb 177
dung 59, 309
dungheap 660, 799
dunghill 109, 253
ear 194, 201, 383, 476, 543, 1060
early-riser 647, 999
east 944

easygoing 389
eat (to) 319, 359, 482, 492, 710, 1110
economy 285–6
edge 1016
education 287–91
efficiency 873
effort 292–6
egg 37, 204, 704
egotism 297
elbow 1103
eloquence 298
embers 432
empty 918
empty (to) 793
end 284, 513, 540, 747, 960, 1068
endure 299, 869
enemy 419, 422, 1031, 1109
English 300, 1074
Englishman 70, 1134
envy 609
equality 301–5
error 306, 1110, 1135
evening 1008, 1011
everyone 740
everything 904
evidence 1131
evil 307–12, 469, 597, 635, 1111
exchange 105
excuse 313–15, 985–96
expect (to) 445, 705
experience 316–27

eye 82, 87, 194, 226, 305, 402, 451, 550, 632, 644, 680, 702, 748, 781, 880, 886, 1035, 1057, 1060, 1103, 1112
face 232
fail (to) 387, 745
fair 328, 1049
fair-haired 328
fall 237
fall (to) 331, 346, 381, 618, 730, 796
fall out (to) 144
falsehood 1124
falsify (to) 806
fame 329–32
familiarity 333–6
family 645, 1084
famine 1029
farmer 1104
farthing 562
fat 200, 249, 874
fate 337–46
father 164, 699, 887
fault 148, 306, 634, 643, 683, 956, 966
fear 111, 255, 338, 347–9, 955
feast 497, 503, 747
feed 156
feel (to) 308, 849
fence 838–40, 1039–40
ferry 133
fever 509

Fianna 1132

field 139, 657, 791

fight (to) 350–7, 435, 618, 746–7, 1084

fill (to) 686, 793

find (to) 321

finger 75, 166, 495

fire 124, 136, 190, 397, 479, 494, 827, 995, 1029, 1031, 1124, 1127

fireside 519

first 123, 125, 128, 165, 237, 363

fish 538–9, 789

fist 90, 151, 565, 857, 1117

fit (to) 877

flail 1037, 1116

flattery 358

flea 420, 785, 1109

flesh 33, 1055, 1062

flimsiness 359

flock 399, 507

flood 135, 533, 808

floor 718

flower 60

foal 557, 1042, 1093

foliage 346, 715

follow (to) 114, 711, 858

folly 381, 907

fond 646

food 186, 360–5, 561, 683, 724, 888, 953, 984, 1055, 1111, 1113

fool 8, 13, 57, 366–77, 926, 984, 1091–2

foolishness 164, 291, 368–82

foot 169, 264, 320, 346, 499, 241, 296, 553, 556, 659, 781, 817, 885, 888, 1049

forbearance 733

force 786, 1127

ford 135, 321, 792, 808

forehead 1058

forever 465

forget (to) 25, 243, 400, 482

forgetfulness 1038

forgiveness 383

fortunate 1054, 1131

fortune 384–91, 1038–40, 1135

four 1137–40

fox 48, 80, 202, 870–1, 905, 1059, 1095, 1112

frail 392

freedom 393–4

Frenchmen 1133

fresh 62, 1110

friar 156, 176

Friday 1123

friend 395, 401–2, 404, 408, 415, 425–6, 655, 836, 1031, 1033

friendly 336, 990

friendship 395–427

frieze 1029

front 119

frosty 1029

fruit 560, 828–9

full 140, 187, 483, 486

funeral 856

furrow 1097

futility 428–42

gain 857

gallop 766

gamble (to) 443–5

game 198

gander 302

garden 1050

gathering 855, 1013

generation 959

generosity 184, 446–52, 582, 1032, 1072

gentleness 129, 453–4, 1048

gift 450–1, 481

girl 69, 169, 1035, 1057, 1112, 1129

give (to) 345, 370

glass 1114

glen 1112

goat 45, 174, 434, 712, 990, 1049, 1056, 1101, 1115

gobadán 7

God 90–1, 100, 235, 258, 455–68, 485, 523, 535, 621, 662,

955, 1047

godparents 660

gold 78, 371, 415, 946, 981

good 78, 148, 152, 154–5, 157, 460, 462, 848, 1029–30, 1080

goodness 469–75

goose 160, 178, 302, 704, 870, 871, 970, 982, 990, 1054, 1100

gosling 1027

gospel 67

gossip 476–9

grace 91, 458, 47, 1066

grain 921, 1057

grass 359, 529, 553

gratitude 480–5

grave 227, 659

graveyard 239

greatness 332

greed 486–95, 1133

green 430, 791

grey 98, 236

greyhound 888

grief 496–9

grind (to) 1110

ground 466

grow (to) 627

growl 484

growth 239, 1027

grudge 242

grunt 705

guard (to) 286

guide 462

guilty 580, 862

guinea 1080

guest 416

gurnet 1101

habit 1114

hag 587

haggard 1079

hair 98, 515, 976

hairless 1062

hairy 80

hake 295

half 153, 762

half-word 288

hammer 981, 1116–17

hand 90, 118, 129, 151, 158, 231, 235, 264, 296, 423, 573, 684–5, 717, 758, 760, 786, 1030

handfuls 1020

handsome 36, 386, 1085

handstaff 718

hang (to) 230, 338, 571, 580, 887

happiness 500

harbour 342

hard 47, 103, 291, 1041–2

hare 66, 233, 437, 711, 1095, 1060, 1126

harm 267, 442, 868, 989

harrow 557

haste 678

hatch (to) 788

hate 643, 1127, 1136

hawk 565, 1112

haws 828

hay 199, 997

Hayes, Atty 45

hazel 718

head 80, 101, 234, 236, 298, 326, 349, 430, 543, 569, 668, 811, 867, 885, 951, 958, 1083, 1101, 1113

health 93, 270, 501–18

hear (to) 120, 863, 882, 884

heart 89, 328, 471, 530, 573, 629, 632, 640–1, 644, 646, 850, 904, 940, 1111, 1132

heart-burn 209

hearth 17

Heaven 99, 737

heavy 940, 496

heel 480, 569, 578, 968

heifer 968, 976

heighten (to) 696

Hell 47, 447, 599, 765, 776, 1087

help 361, 424, 455, 464

hen 37, 178, 492, 608, 617, 967, 1048, 1077, 1082

herb 224, 429, 800

herring 923, 1113

hill 50, 172, 418, 476, 980, 1060, 1126

hilltop 17

hide 200, 635, 703

hips 770

historian 628

hoarder 895

hob 47

hog 1107

hole 525

holly 89, 718

holy water 269

home 16, 159, 323, 519–20, 552, 880, 1033, 1081

honest 111, 521–4, 963

honey 487

honour 525–8

hoof 103, 1074, 1099, 1134

hook 139, 294, 314

hope 227, 443, 517, 529–41

horn 54, 117, 251, 260, 1074, 1099, 1134

horse 103, 105, 220, 263, 299, 313, 383, 394, 433, 481, 491, 529, 694, 926, 1000, 1004, 1024, 1046, 1063–4, 1067–8, 1074, 1088, 1103–4, 1134, 1136

horseback 765–6

horseman 196

hospital 16

hot 30, 123, 567

hound 5, 58, 109, 327, 429, 549, 637, 711, 832, 889, 920, 1077, 1091, 1095, 1105, 1136

hour 341

house 18, 136, 146, 333, 380, 434, 485, 637, 687, 749, 891, 903, 928, 936, 967, 1068, 1070, 1076, 1085, 1100, 1111, 1121

housewife 1038, 1102, 1135

howl (to) 1077

humility 542–3

humour 544–5

hunger 546–51, 771

hunt 327

hut 939

hurler 197

husband 657, 667, 1046

idle 479, 552–7, 928

ignominy 635

ignorance 558, 577

illness 297, 512, 518

image 229

impartial 636

impossibility 559

improve 474

inch 32, 169, 449, 500, 572

independence 560

industry 1079

inequality 561–2

initiative 563–8

innocent 580

intelligence 569

intention 537

intervene 1131

intimate 180

invitation 1034

involvement 570–2

Ireland 91, 853, 1116

Irish 82

Irishman 573–6, 688, 1134

iron 494, 577

ivy 89

jackass 379, 440

jaw 725

Jerusalem 739

jewel 86

jigs 414

job 560, 1117

joke 599

journey 97

judge 87, 391, 580, 636

judgement 577–8

juice 360

jump (to) 799, 1126

justice 579–84

keep (to) 859

Kerry 585, 945

kettle 899

kick (to) 352, 823

kid 1056

Kilkenny 350
kill (to) 124, 345, 505, 648, 901
kiln 428, 504
kiln-cast 830
kind 454, 586–7, 1043–8
king 31, 301, 305, 504, 508, 562, 724, 959
kingfisher 7
kinship 588–584
kiss 244, 894
kitchen 544
kitten 212, 1056
knead (to) 943
knee 1103, 1105
knot 128, 137
know (to) 333, 921–2
knowledge 430, 595–8
labour 874, 1014, 1053
lad 169
ladle 613
lady 1067
lake 1100
lamb 230, 577, 701, 990, 1048
lame 398
land 789, 1095
lark 71, 216, 713
last 125, 337
last (to) 329, 654
late 240, 472
laugh 28, 163, 369, 502, 545, 750, 907, 1134
lavender 252

law 102, 558, 583, 599–604, 721, 756, 873
lazy 74–5, 605–17
leadership 618
leaky 1070
leap 126, 390, 600
learn (to) 287–9, 325, 1018
least 143, 744
leathers 925
leave (to) 632, 1066
leg 115, 130, 717, 971
leisure 678
liar 593, 914
liberty 198
lick (to) 488
lie 245, 505, 619–21
lie (to) 234, 252, 512, 604, 1133
life 225, 329, 345, 527, 622–8, 969, 1098
light 289, 371
lily 63
limb 1132
lime 817
lion 219, 763
lips 132, 640, 666
listen (to) 39, 825
litter 395 790, 800
little 75, 141, 154, 158, 448, 473
live (to) 20, 92, 333, 594, 622–3, 626, 629
liveliest 891

load 1020
loaf 762
loan 104, 106, 682, 755, 761
lodging 149
lonesome 27, 671
long 49, 158, 323, 329, 337
look 119, 133, 126, 138, 301
loose 115
Lord (the) 440, 561
lose (to) 107, 116, 128, 176, 263, 294, 313, 342, 527
louder 476
Lough Sheelin 279
louse 200
love 462, 542, 629–46, 1090, 1093
lowly 234
luck 94, 100, 281, 376, 384, 386, 390, 647–54, 658, 967, 1039–40, 1129
luidín 75
lump 182
lurk 232
mac Cumhaill, Fionn 72
mackerel 1094
mad 1129
madman 144
maid 195
make (to) 752

mangy 1062

manners 655–6, 887

mare 1042, 1054, 1093

market 200

market-women 681

marriage 94, 478,
    657–78, 1076

marrow 714, 1055

mason 1017, 1108

mass 269, 1034, 1066,
    1086, 1123

master 317

maturity 679

may 60

meal 523, 943

meanness 184, 286,
    680–5

meat 876

Meath 989

meet (to) 348, 452, 652,
    1112, 1129

meitheal 56

melodious 71

melody 1119

men 686, 1044–6, 1106

mend (to) 143, 744

merriment 579

message 870

messenger 611, 615,
    905

mickle 1005

midden 931

midge 680

mile 572

milestone 414

milk 53, 831, 835, 1135

mill 428, 1000, 1034,
    1119

miller 523, 1108

mim 42

mind 306, 594, 1053

mirror 402

misery 531

misfortune 517,
    687–96, 937

mistakes 368

misty 833

modesty 332

money 274, 330, 366,
    457, 515, 585, 677,
    1033, 1088, 1120,
    1129

money-maker 935

moon 595, 658, 931

moor 832

moorhen 1113

morning 269, 649, 801,
    1008, 1040, 1129–30

mote 252

mother 164, 168, 630,
    697–9

mountain 418, 548,
    594, 672, 773, 779

mountainy 672

mouse 710, 1121

mouth 89, 129, 140,
    142, 227, 454, 535,
    722, 850, 861–4,
    868, 881, 951

mow (to) 998

mud 367, 1095–6

mule 1052

Mullingar 968

mungret 46

music 784

musical 861

mustard 548

nail 1035, 1057

name 152, 815

native 20, 740

nature 700–17, 1125

neatness 718

necessity 719–23

neck 170, 1058

need 259

neighbour 136, 1040

nest 201, 616

new 146, 480

news 95, 697

niggardly 286

night 337, 344, 541,
    1114, 1135

nimble 233

nobility 39, 724

noble 1067

nobody 741

nod 433

noise 247, 865

Nora 476

north 692

nose 32, 881

nothing 334, 685

nourishing 1055

nun 182

nurse (to) 339

nursling 339
nurture 707
oak 846
oaten 1093
oath 585, 1120
obedience 725
obligations 726
ocean 435, 946
oinseach 375, 377
old 23, 25–7, 38, 45, 50, 61, 232, 242, 280, 478, 518, 731
olive 360
O'Neill 451
one 116
opinion 929
ordinance 558
otter 1087
outline 814
own 757
ownership 727
packsaddle 755
Paddy 252
pain 85, 430, 797
pair 925
palace 939
paper 142
parish 177, 1035
parsnips 358
participation 728
patch 525
path 320
patience 729–39
patient 510, 802
patriotism 740

paw 487
pay (to) 243, 271, 285, 516
payment 272
peace 575, 741–7
peacemaker 745
pen 142
penny 411, 570, 782
people 117, 336
perception 748–9
perish 217
person 31, 219, 356, 391, 461
pessimist 147
pet 181, 1069
physician 222, 503, 517, 531
pie 495
piece 473
pig 8, 130, 175, 181, 252, 523, 568, 592, 705, 708, 743, 990, 1002, 1048, 1052, 1069, 1104
pin 961
pinch 318
pipe 988, 1114
piper 75, 1115
pitcher 343
pity 340, 424, 427, 612, 726, 750–1, 929
place 542, 878, 1122
plaster 668, 735
plate 975
play 728

pleasant 1056
pleasure 24, 659
pleasure-seeker 1044
pledge 585
plough 1119
ploughing 1100
ploughshare 1097
ploughteam 699
plover 520
pocket 425, 1080, 1130
poem 752
poetry 752, 1072
point 392
poison 876
poker 40
poor 562, 939, 1047
Pope 971
porridge 132, 175
possession 753–64, 1120
postpone (to) 157, 801
pot 83, 115, 363, 764
potato 477, 1050, 1071
pouch 699
pound 570, 601
poverty 765–85
power 786–7
praise 162, 321, 423, 740, 791, 1023
praiseach 989
precious 528, 625
pressure 586
presumption 778–93
pretty 60
price 922

pride 794–9

priest 178–9, 181, 183, 524, 794, 1035, 1069, 1133

prince 1107

prisoner 31

procrastination 800–2

profit 266, 688

progress 162, 1023

promise 803

proof 319

property 176, 783, 895

prosperity 387, 388–9, 526

protect 275

protruding 666

prove (to) 406

proverbs 804–6

provide (to) 608

Providence 368

prudence 807–9

puck-goat 80

pudding 319

pump 725

pup 327

pupil 290

purity 1132

purpose 896

purr (to) 848

purse 411, 601, 940, 1075

qualities 889

quarrelsome 351

quench (to) 453, 1029

quern 1037

quite 742–3, 1002

rabbit 268, 891

racehorse 440

rafter 230

rag 493

rage 347

ragweed 73

ragworth 73

rain 256, 340, 652, 1031, 1123

ram 54, 1125

raven 211, 639

ray 1094

razor 1051

reaper 314

reaping 314

rear (to) 655, 713

recede (to) 533

recent 496

recognise (to) 401, 588

recompense 443

red hair 810–11, 1063, 1084, 1129

refusal 150, 153

refuse (to) 491, 972

reign 504

rein 263, 926

relapse 509

relationship 407, 498

relative 843

relief 501, 691

remain (to) 666

renew (to) 715

rent 561, 629, 1033, 1073

repentence 812–13

reputation 814–17

resourcefulness 568

rest 145, 221, 627, 1087

return (to) 228, 902, 1086

reveal 273

revenge 818

reverence 396

rich 79, 773

ride (to) 259, 765

right 303

ring 15

ripe 730, 791

rise (to) 331, 384, 1039

river 105, 133, 304

road 149, 183, 218, 323, 1059

rock 199, 594

rod 559, 847

rogue 111, 521, 819–23, 914

roof 380, 1070

root 246

rope 439, 887

rotten 844

row (to) 1117

ruin 443, 845

rumour 824–7

run 292, 299, 978, 1126

rush 392, 990, 1124

rust 1088–9

sack 486

sacrifice 317

saddle 313, 466, 755

sadness 774
safe 914
sale 1050
St Colmcille 983
sallow 471
salmon 294, 764, 1113
salty 77
salutation 504
sand 439
Sassanach 1074
satisfy (to) 759
Saturday 1123
sauce 547
sauciest 1125
Saxon 300, 1074
say (to) 141, 143, 744, 882
scabby 399
scald 132
Scandinavian 1055
scant 697
scarcity 828–30
scar 823
scatter (to) 423, 1013, 1021
scattering 855
scholar 954
school 1086
schoolmaster 1064–7
scold (to) 841, 1070, 1081
scratch (to) 617
scythe 1051
sea 68, 77, 227–8, 439, 539, 764, 773, 787, 1094, 1096

seal 1094
seasons 831–5
seat 579
secret 275, 836–43
secure (to) 1034
security 585
see 120, 167, 722, 884, 1090
seed 1033
seek (to) 996, 1057
seldom 246
select (to) 1042, 1051
self-destruction 844–7
selfishness 848–53
sell (to) 202, 468, 491
sense 325, 382, 854, 872, 961, 991, 1083
separation 412, 855
settlement 633
severe 456
shabby 1024
shadow 626, 974
shake 237
shallow 247
shame 738, 778, 780, 856–8, 916–17, 972
shamefaced 934
shameless 277, 1048, 1062
share 189, 557, 650, 851
sharp 52, 57–8, 550, 987, 1091–2
sheaf 718
shed (to) 1025

sheep 101, 24, 359, 399, 571, 701, 831, 990, 1036, 1042, 1082
shilling 562
shin 131, 606, 609
ship 116, 342, 504, 1050, 1096
shirt 671, 1046, 1080
shoe 38, 318, 1088
shop 270
shore 980
short 265, 323
shot 648
shoulders 33, 326, 426, 606, 958, 1015
shout 476
show (to) 249
shower 945–6
shrew 993
shy 662, 821, 860, 972
shyness 859–60
sickle 990
sickness 503
side 304, 408
sigh 450
sight 632, 781, 1035, 1038, 1135
signify (to) 596
sign 1131
silence 861–8
silk 712
sin 798
sing (to) 890
single 941
sink (to) 1068

sit (to) 409, 480, 878
skill 1126
skin 84, 200, 202, 230, 417, 700, 995, 1025
sky 216
slate 380
sleep 229, 502, 504, 607, 690, 1040, 1071
sleepy-head 990
slender 1061
slip 306
slipper 663
slippery 936
sloven 657
slow 64, 320, 432, 889
small 1036
smile 1074
smear (to) 310
smith 56
smoke 827, 1109
smoke (to) 1114
smoky 785, 1070, 1081
snail 738
snarl 1134
snout 80, 1104-5
soft 358
soldier 1064
sole 264, 925
somebody 333
son 164, 166, 171, 374, 444, 724
soon 143, 744
soothe (to) 530, 795, 864
sores 735

sorrow 164, 274, 500, 696, 932
sorry (to be) 127, 813, 678
sound 1037, 1038
sour 272
source 289
sow 405, 998, 1054
spade 1089
spancel 726
speak 126, 297, 686, 694, 697, 885, 952
speckled 606, 609
speed 1006, 1008
spender 895
spill (to) 396
spin (to) 1100
spit 100, 268, 413, 574
spiteful 906
split (to) 846
spoil (to) 752
spoon 932
sprat 295
spread (to) 309
spring 609, 833-4, 1033
spring (to) 307
spuds 785
spur 347, 352, 569
spy (to) 901
squalling 1081
stain 310
stand (to) 292, 436
star 865
stay (to) 1120
steal (to) 522

step 1059
stick 206
stiff 40
still 248
sting 246
stingy 683
stitch 128, 134, 614
stocking 310, 663
stomach 551, 852
stone 113, 206, 504, 930, 1043, 1083, 1097
stool 131, 480
store 655
storm 340, 532
story 191, 265, 315, 546, 824-5, 910
storyteller 900
Strabane 619
straddle 755
straight 261
strange 683
stranger 726
street 18, 903
strength 97, 205, 869, 1132
stretch 187, 296
strike (to) 349, 353, 484, 566-7, 570, 1120, 1116
strong 6, 498, 707, 116-17
stubborn 990
stupidity 870-2
sty 743, 790, 809

succeed (to) 745
success 445, 873–4
suffer (to) 745, 993
sufficient 189, 293
suit (to) 467
suitability 875–7
suitor 195
summer 250
summit 172
sun 17, 168, 532
Sunday 50, 1042, 1086, 1123
sunlight 652
sunrise 1128
sunset 1128
sunshine 1032, 340
suppose (to) 254
sure 127, 746
surplus 1033
survive (to) 1093
swallow 250
swamp 220
swear (to) 1120
sweep (to) 146
sweet 246, 271–2, 419, 488, 624, 938, 1003
sweetheart 1057
swift 66, 1094–5
sword 1030, 1089
table 88, 178, 361, 1066
tact 878–87
tail 42, 703, 975
tailor 614, 1115
take (to) 285, 877
tale 826

talent 888–91
talk 185, 192–3, 198, 442, 463, 479, 552, 598, 866, 892–4, 1009, 1046
tame 704
taste 345, 829
tattered 1046
tax 192
teach 21, 290–1, 461, 1052
teeth 58, 122, 137, 481, 1065
tell (to) 477, 916
temper 964
tenant 928
thank (to) 480, 485
thatch 380, 428, 875
thief 522, 591, 776, 1107
thieving 80, 1084
think 126
thirst 274, 277, 283–4
thistle 17
thong 34
thorn 367, 1049, 1091–2
thought 1089
thread 1092
three 97, 100, 138, 659, 1029–132
threshing 1116
thrift 895–7
throat 213, 883
thrush 1113

tide 7, 538, 564, 658, 1053
tie 128, 137
tight 681
time 134, 215, 739, 898–900
tiniest 307
tip 318
tire (to) 935
tit 976
tithes 516
Toal 43
tobacco 186
today 465, 1007
toe 725
toil 659
tomorrow 1007
tongue 117, 137, 246, 298, 306, 315, 621, 725, 883, 913, 987, 1065, 1088
tonight 1008
tool 1016
tooth 1091, 1099
tough 41
trace 231, 1096–7
track 1041
trade 317, 336
traits 1058–61
trample 309
trashbag 681
treachery 70, 901–2
treat (to) 280
tree 188, 237, 346, 357, 737, 844, 846, 1112

trials 669

trifle 369, 757

trouble 24, 213, 401,
414, 858, 903–4,
983, 1108

trout 764

true 67

trumpet 1065

trust 905–6, 979,
1098–9, 1134

truth 273, 620, 907–17,
1128

tune 782

tuppence 681

turf 552, 779

turn 135, 1126

turnip 438

twelve 1133

twenty 627

twig 19

twist (to) 559

two 119, 134, 148, 181,
220, 241, 356, 451,
470, 569, 574, 749,
760, 891

ugly 386, 1030, 1062–3

understand (to) 288,
852, 918–19, 1045,
1053

unfortunate 386

unknown 320

unruly 1048

unstable 1043

useless 920–4, 1064–5

valley 430

value 35, 922, 925–8,
941, 1100–1

vanity 929–31

vessel 4

vigilance 1039, 1079

vigour 1117

village 857

virtue 720, 738, 800,
1130

visit 879, 1040

voice 96, 938, 1072

waist 1061

walk 398, 1058, 1135

wall 431

wander 1026

want 489, 753, 757

warm 190, 378, 587,
675

warning 353, 932

washing 671

waste 152, 432, 933

watch (to) 728

water 34, 65, 160,
247–8, 278, 338,
343, 589, 723, 807,
1029, 1043, 1124,
1127, 1135

waterfall 1041, 1087

wax 1043

weak 6

weakling 362

weaken (to) 586

wealth 506, 934–43

weapon 836

wearer 318

weather 944–6, 997

weave 339

web 339

wedge 846

welcome 416, 947–9

well 394, 723, 1021

wet 49, 59

wheat 921

wheel 786

wheelstring 41

whelp 549

whey 173

whiskey 269–70, 511

whisper 476

whistle 2, 414, 920,
1007, 1077

white 37, 310, 639, 694,
1046, 1063, 1068,
1085

wicked 964, 1118

wide 448

widow 950, 1056

width 304

wife 194, 278, 604,
659, 661, 665–8,
670, 674, 950, 1030,
1046, 1066, 1070,
1136

wild 704

will 465

win 263

wind 354, 388, 875,
944, 957, 1031,
1090, 1109

wine 273, 355

wink 433

winter 605, 833, 835

wisdom 779, 951–62, 1032, 1136

wise 14, 46, 164, 651, 867

wish 993

wisp 924

witness 245, 604

wolf 974, 1065

woman 31, 46, 82, 161, 182, 280, 282, 477–9, 638, 662, 672–3, 677, 794, 810, 841, 963–93, 1036, 1042, 1045, 1048, 1049–53, 1061, 1063, 1066–7, 1071, 1077, 1082–3, 1085, 1088, 1093, 1096, 1100, 1105, 1121

wood 715, 844, 1097

woodcock 1101

wooden 1030

wool 434, 1100

woollen 1092

words 156, 161, 354, 356, 358, 367, 454, 601, 864, 1091, 1098, 1132

work 57, 145, 362–3, 994–1022, 1086

worker 1044

workhouse 363

world 393, 608, 665, 950, 1115, 1047

worst 1066–71

wound 849

wren 124, 758

wretched 422

writing 1098

wrong 31

year 536, 623

yellow 73, 328, 1063, 1133

yesterday 465

yield (to) 300

young 25, 232, 291, 478, 710, 1056

youth 24, 25, 1023–8